# TRADING
## STRATEGIES

**DAY TRADING + SWING TRADING**

A Beginner's Guide to Trading with Easy and Replicable Strategies to Maximize Your
Profit. How to Use Tools, Techniques, Risk Management, and Mindset

# MARK SWING

**© Copyright 2021 by Mark Swing - All rights reserved.**

This Book is provided with the sole purpose of providing relevant information on a specific topic for which every reasonable effort has been made to ensure that it is both accurate and reasonable. Nevertheless, by purchasing this Book you consent to the fact that the author, as well as the publisher, are in no way experts on the topics contained herein, regardless of any claims as such that may be made within. As such, any suggestions or recommendations that are made within are done so purely for entertainment value. It is recommended that you always consult a professional prior to undertaking any of the advice or techniques discussed within.

This is a legally binding declaration that is considered both valid and fair by both the Committee of Publishers Association and the American Bar Association and should be considered as legally binding within the United States.

The reproduction, transmission, and duplication of any of the content found herein, including any specific or extended information will be done as an illegal act regardless of the end form the information ultimately takes. This includes copied versions of the work both physical, digital, and audio unless express consent of the Publisher is provided beforehand. Any additional rights reserved.

Furthermore, the information that can be found within the pages described forthwith shall be considered both accurate and truthful when it comes to the recounting of facts. As such, any use, correct or incorrect, of the provided information will render the Publisher free of responsibility as to the actions taken outside of their direct purview. Regardless, there are zero scenarios where the original author or the Publisher can be deemed liable in any fashion for any damages or hardships that may result from any of the information discussed herein.

Additionally, the information in the following pages is intended only for informational purposes and should thus be thought of as universal. As befitting its nature, it is presented without assurance regarding its prolonged validity or interim quality. Trademarks that are mentioned are done without written consent and can in no way be considered an endorsement from the trademark holder.

# STOP

## TAKE YOUR GIFT

As a way of saying thanks for your purchase, I'm offering an **EXTRA BONUS**:

Glossary of useful terms linked to markets in financial instruments

Scan the QR Code with your mobile phone and request your **GIFT now!**

# TABLE OF CONTENTS

## BOOK 2: SWING TRADING STRATEGIES

# DAY TRADING

Quickstart Guide for Beginners with Powerful Strategies to Trade Options, Stocks, Forex, Futures, Crypto, and ETFs to Generate a Continuous Cash Flow

**MARK SWING**

# >> INTRODUCTION <<

Congratulations on downloading *Day Trading: Quickstart Guide for Beginners with Powerful Strategies to Trade Options, Stocks, Forex, Futures, Crypto, and ETFs to Generate a Continuous Cash Flow*, and thank you for doing so. This is a book that I have written in a series of six. My objective is to transform any beginner investor into a successful trader in all types of financial trading, real estate, or dividend stocks by guiding them on how to make their first steps and get into the required momentum. To that effect, I have published six books, and the one you are about to read is number three in the series. In case you enjoy reading this one, which I am sure you will, feel free to download the others, as they will be just as engaging and informative. I will list them at the end of your read, together with the links where you can download them.

Now, the trading of financial assets has been growing tremendously this decade due to more exposure of people to the art. This is the decade when small-scale traders and individuals have been enabled to trade. In the past, trading was reserved for the big boys and institutions who could afford the hefty requirements, such as capital running into the millions of dollars. Today, thanks to brokers and the use of something called leverage, which we are going to discuss later, anybody can trade with only a smartphone, computer, and a few dollars.

As the industry grows, so has false information. One of the biggest lies being thrown at innocent would-be traders is that it is an easy art. Assuming that you have not traded before, you might have already come across an online ad telling you, "Trading is easy. Just do ABC, and you will be making millions in a month!" If you have ever been curious enough to follow through with such an advert to the end, their objective is usually, "Sign up with us to start your journey into the millionaires' club." It is all pure marketing fluff.

Make no mistake; trading can be made simple, but it is not easy! As much as there are tons of websites and intruding ads that try to make you believe this misconception, any established trader like me will advise you otherwise. Typically, ads will make you believe that after reading a few books or paying for some over-promising online courses, you will automatically transform into a successful professional trader.

## WRONG!

To be on the safe side, perceive any form of trading like any other profession you know. You can neither become an engineer by skimming through 200 pages of an expensive book sold on Amazon nor can you qualify to be a doctor in a week, no matter how intense your training is. In the same way, trading of any kind requires serious education before anyone can put their money on the line and start reaping profits from it. Trading, when properly done, can earn you more money than some of the best careers that you know. Ask yourself, then, how you can make more money than someone who has studied for years, yet all you did was to enroll in a 2-month course or buy a magical trading system for a couple of dollars?

To cut the long story short, congratulations for thinking differently. The reason you have decided to purchase this quick-start guide to day trading is that you understand the seriousness that trading requires. Fortunately for you, by the end of your reading, you will understand all the necessary concepts to get you started on the journey of becoming a profitable trader. That is exactly what this book was created to do. However, keep in mind that reading it will not make you successful instantaneously. Rather, it will get you started in the long journey toward understanding day trading, and, with time, you will become the successful trader that everyone dreams of becoming.

That said, here is an overview of what the chapters inside the book will look like:

- Chapter 1 will kick-start your journey to successful trading by elaborating on the meaning of online trading. In addition to the definition, we shall see the different types of online trading that exist and how to settle for the best ones.

- In Chapter 2, we are going to look at one of the markets that we shall base most of our strategies on—the forex market. This is the biggest market in the world, and, by using it as our basis for this book, we can apply the same concepts in the other markets. It is important to understand what a market entails, how it works, and the role that we play in it for us to generate consistent profits.

- Chapter 3 will highlight the four styles used in trading. These styles determine how much time a trader uses them on their platforms. This is an important chapter in which it tells us why we should opt for day trading in making a living as opposed to the other three.

- Chapter 4 will outline the basic tools that a person needs in order to start trading effectively.

- Chapter 5 contains the basic and most important words and phrases used in the online trading industry. By understanding these words, the learning experience becomes simplified and more enjoyable.

- In Chapter 6, we shall discuss some of the most common trading platforms used in online trading. In addition, we are going to look at the MT5, which we shall use for our study, in terms of installation and some types of charts found in it.

- Chapter 7 will present yet another controversial debate that begs the question, "Which one between fundamental and technical market analysis is better?" It will explain the two approaches in detail and explain why we shall choose one of them for our day trading guide.

- In chapter 8, we are going to get started with the most interesting and important approach to analyze the charts and know whether to sell or buy an instrument. We shall study the anatomy of candlesticks and what they mean. In addition, the chapter will reveal the basic but very profitable candlestick patterns used in day trading.

- Chapter 9 will talk about another crucial concept of trading known as support and resistance. These are important areas that every trader needs to be familiar with as they help them in making decisions about the management of their trades.

- Chapter 10 is about chart indicators. Unlike the two concepts discussed in chapters 8 and 9 that depend on the trader's skill, chapter 10 will introduce some automated analytic tools. These tools will help the trader to spot important information that can add to the accuracy of their signals.

- In chapter 11, we shall introduce another magical concept, which helps traders in predicting the future of the market, known as Elliot Waves. This approach is used by the best traders in the world. However, to some junior traders, it appears like a tough concept to grasp. In this guide, Elliot Waves have been laid out in simple terms so the reader can understand them and use them in their analysis with ease and accuracy.

- Chapter 12 introduces yet another popular day trading pattern that can be used in any type of market. It is similar to the Elliot Waves but has fewer waves and requires the use of an additional tool known as Fibonacci for proper analysis.

- The second-last chapter, Chapter 13, will discuss risk management. These are the proven ways that a practicing trader can minimize their losses and boost their profits in the high-risk environment of trading.

- Finally, our last chapter will discuss the final tool that a trader needs: a trading plan. This is the one tool that brings the trader life and keeps it in perfect order.

There are plenty of books on this subject on the market, so thanks again for choosing this one. Every effort was made to ensure it is full of as much useful information as possible. Please enjoy!

## IMPORTANT!

Please note that day trading, like any other form of trading, is a high-risk venture. The investment or capital that you use is in trading is always at a risk of loss. Second, trading leveraged financial instruments might not be favorable for everyone. Therefore, even as you venture into online trading, make sure you have implemented the risk-managing fundamentals recommended in this book. Finally, only risk the money that you are comfortable losing.

# CHAPTER 1
## WHAT IS ONLINE TRADING?

Well, we are already getting started with our day trading guide. In this chapter, we are going to define the phrase "day trading" so that everyone, especially those who have never come across trading, can grasp what trading entails. As promised, this book will start you off in the context of day trading from the lowest point possible and let you go when you can successfully trade any financial asset and make profits. As such, in case you are a seasoned trader who is only interested in the day trading strategies, you might consider skipping a few chapters ahead. However, I would recommend that you skim through the earlier chapters as you might pick a tip or two that would enhance your trading experience.

### DEFINITION OF ONLINE TRADING

In the simplest terms, trading is something that we do every day, although we might not refer to it that way. Whenever you exchange something in return for another, you have executed a trade. For example, when it is hot, you get some money and buy yourself some ice cream to cool yourself down. In that scenario, you have exchanged your money in return for the ice cream. The vendor, too, has given you the ice cream in exchange for your money. So, in short, we can refer to trading as the purchase and/or selling of services and goods with compensation paid to a seller by a buyer.

The same concept applies to the online trading of securities. You may get confused by this word. A "security" is any tradable financial asset. There are three categories of securities:

- Equity securities such as stocks

- Debt securities such as banknotes, cryptocurrency, and bonds

- Derivates such as options and futures

You will get to understand them better as we go along. Everything that we are going to trade and discuss falls under one of the above categories.

Trading any financial asset follows the same concept as purchasing ice cream; only this time, no physical goods or services are involved. Let us take stocks, for example. If Facebook is selling a single stock at $180, it means anyone who can afford that money can own a piece of the company. If the company's overall worth grows, so will the value of its stocks. So, if someone had bought the stock for $180 and it appreciated to $185, then they can sell the stock and make a profit of $5 for each stock they held. Remember that all this happened without them contacting or even going to Facebook. Do you get it now?

From the above explanation, we can now define online trading as the act of buying and selling financial assets (or products) over the internet. Traders, both buyers and sellers, need an online platform that brings them together and enables their exchange to happen. In online trading, financial instruments like stocks, cryptocurrency, international currencies, futures, options, and Exchange-Traded-Funds (ETFs) are involved. The internet acts as the channel through which buyers and sellers meet. The marketplace is created by intermediary parties known as "brokers." These are the firms that create trading platforms on the web and enable the exchange between the two parties to happen.

In the days before the internet was born, investors had to visit their brokers physically or make calls to them. The brokers would provide the investors with information, such as the trading time and the price of the requested financial instruments. After this, the investor would decide whether to purchase the instruments or not. If they wanted to buy them, they would tell the brokers to place the orders for them. Once they had made some profits, it was the broker who would get the money and pay the traders physically. If the traders made losses, they would give the money to the brokers to deposit it for them, so they could trade again in the future. This is how lengthy and tedious traditional trading was before the internet age.

Today, trading has become a self-service. An investor can do everything from the comfort of their home. With a computer, anyone can access market information, deposit their money, execute trades, and withdraw their profits without involving any third parties. However, a broker is necessary since they provide the platforms required for these processes.

## TYPES OF TRADING MARKETS

As you might have noticed, trading is a very wide industry. By the time you finally decide to start day trading, you must have decided on the type of market or markets that you will be trading. This is because each market behaves differently and might have unique requirements. All the same, the methods of trading that you will learn can be applied in any market that you choose. The main differences between different markets lie in the type of asset that is being traded, the volume of the assets (size of the market), volatility (the rate of price changes), and the amount of investment capital required.

Let us look at some of the major markets that you can choose from.

## 1. The Forex Market

The forex market is the biggest financial market in the world today. The name "forex" is coined from the words "Foreign" and "Exchange." In essence, when trading forex, you are simply making money by exchanging one currency for another. For instance, you can use US Dollars to purchased Japanese Yen (JPY). When the value of the USD increases or that of the JPY decreases, you can make profits from that exchange. We are going to delve deeper into the forex market as it will form the basis of our strategies since it is the most traded market in the world, and the strategies applied in trading currencies can be used in any other market.

## 2. The Stock Market

The stock market is the oldest financial market that has been in existence decades before the forex market was born. Today, it is still very popular despite trailing the forex market by far. When trading the stock market, you are simply buying and selling the shares of a particular company such as Google, Amazon, Shell, Facebook, Bing, and so on. In addition to the shares, stock trading also allows the trading of indices like:

- *DAX 30:* This is a collection of the top 30 companies in Germany that are listed on the Frankfurt Stock Exchange.

- *FTSE 100:* This is a collection of the top 100 companies listed on the London Stock Exchange.

- *S&P 500:* This is a collection of the top 100 of the most traded stocks (shares) in the United States.

- **Dow Jones:** This is a collection of 30 of the biggest and most influential companies in the United States.

- **Hang-Seng:** This is a collection of the 50 top-ranked companies listed on the Hong Kong Stock Exchange.

- **NASDAQ Composite:** This is a collection of the world's leading tech companies.

Stock trading has fiercer competition compared to forex. Again, depending on the country where one is based, they might be required to hold a minimal amount of money as capital. In the US, for instance, one should have at least $25,000 in their account. Due to this, trading stocks might be unfavorable for beginners who have limited capital.

## 3. The Futures Market

Just like the name suggests, the futures market involves making trades for the future. Better put, they are a form of contract where a seller and a buyer agree to execute a trade at a specific date and price in the future. Futures trading mostly involves commodities like precious metals, oil, and foods.

The idea of futures contracts is to minimize risk and unpredictability. For example, if you knew that in a few weeks' time, you would have dug 1 kilogram of gold, you can agree with a buyer to buy it at the current price of gold, as long as it is profitable for you. When you have the gold in hand, you will get the price that you had agreed on whether the price of gold at present went up or fell. In this way, profits are guaranteed, and the risk is minimized.

Similarly, in the futures market, you purchase a financial asset online and only sell it after a specified time or after it attains a specific value in the future.

Just like stock markets, trading futures requires a lot more money than forex and some of the other markets. On average, you need a few thousand dollars to be able to trade, although this varies with the type of future contract that you choose. For instance, you need at least $3,500 to trade the S&P 500. Flexibility is also low since one might be required to close one contract before executing another.

## 4. The Options Market

Options markets are quite new compared to the three markets above. Options are straightforward financial derivates where a contract allows the trader to buy or sell an instrument within or during a pre-determined time. It is the seller's obligation to fulfill the transaction by either buying or selling their instruments before the set expiration date.

Options trading is considered risky because of the fixed expiration. When executing an options trade, one can either CALL, which means buying at the current price, or PUT, which means selling at the current price.

Examples of tradable options include mini options, index options, stock options, S&P options, and so on. However, some of these instruments might not be possible when day trading.

## 5. The Crypto Market

The cryptocurrency market is the newest type of online trading. Cryptocurrency refers to digital money that is based on the internet and uses cryptographical functions to enable financial transactions. Since this currency is not regulated, it tends to be rather risky and prone to fluctuations. All the same, it has gained significant popularity recently and continues to rise. Therefore, it can be traded like fiat currencies.

Bitcoin is the most popular and valuable cryptocurrency at the time of writing this book. Other cryptos include Dash, Ethereum, Ripple, and Litecoin. These can be traded similar to the forex markets since they are forms of money; that is, you can make profits by exchanging currency with cryptocurrency.

The cryptocurrency market is becoming a large entity in online trading due to several factors. One of them is due to the high volatility of the currencies. The second one is that trading them requires very little capital, just like forex trading. Another reason is that they are easy to access and can be traded without requiring a broker.

### 6. The Binary Options Market

The final type of online trading market that we are going to discuss is known as binary options. It is a rather interesting form of trading in that all you need to do is to predict whether an instrument will trade higher or lower after a certain time. Better put, if the current price of gold is $1,500, you can predict that it will be higher or lower after 15 minutes. If your prediction is correct, then your capital grows. If the prediction is incorrect, then you lose the amount you had staked.

Binary options trading is fast emerging as a favorite market for day traders because of the expiry feature. In addition, one can trade on almost any financial instrument across the market. Another advantage of binary options is that the required capital is very little, as some brokers allow the traders to stake a dollar or less per trade. Finally, this is the only market where a person knows how much they can make or lose even before they execute the trades.

### CHOOSING YOUR MARKET

As stated earlier, the day trading strategies that we are going to study in this book can be used in any type of market. However, it is up to the individual trader to de-cide which type of market they prefer to focus on. You can choose more than one type of market, but it might end up being too tedious and confusing. As such, as we go deeper into the book, you might consider trying the strategies for different markets so that by the end of it, you will have made a decision.

Some factors that might help you in choosing your pre-ferred market are:

- **Accessibility:** Make sure the type of market you choose is available in your country, or there are brokers that you can use. The closer a broker is to your country, the better.

- **Resources:** Different markets have different require-ments. For example, you can trade binary options from a phone, but stocks and forex are best done us-ing a computer. In short, choose what you can com-fortably support.

- **Capital:** This aspect has been mentioned several times already. You should only go for the market that you are sure you can finance without struggling. Forex, crypto and binary options are the best choices if you have little to risk.

- **Volatility:** This is the amount of price fluctuation that an instrument undergoes in a given time. Since we are going to be focusing on day trading, look for markets that move a lot during the day, so you have enough opportunities to make profits.

- **Liquidity:** This is the ability to sell or buy a financial instrument without the price being affected. High liquidity means you can make more trades in a day.

- **Personality:** This is a very important factor to con-sider when choosing your markets. You might find that stocks are more appealing to you than binary options or futures contracts. Choose what you find interesting as it is your first step toward a successful day trading.

To this point, you should have a clear understanding of what makes up online trading and the different markets that you can go for. It might be too early to choose what you want, but things will clear up as we start doing the actual trading, and you practice on some of these markets. If this is the case, let us find out what day trading means in the next chapter.

# CHAPTER 2
## WHAT IS FOREX TRADING?

In the previous chapter, we have seen that the forex market is the biggest and most traded one. We would, therefore, not be wrong to conclude that even a majority of those who will download this book might end up trading in this gigantic market. Well, the point we are trying to drive home here is that the forex market will form the basis of our guide. We shall focus primarily on it, bringing out the strategies that will guarantee our success as day traders.

Like we said earlier, in as much as the stock market, the futures market, the options market, the cryptocurrency market, and the other markets are independent types of trading, they all use the same approach. A good example is that all the charts that we shall use for our analysis in forex day trading will contain what we call candlesticks, fundamental analysis, and indicators. These are helpful in reading the markets and understanding where there is a consistent movement of the price (we call it a trend), where the market is likely to bounce and go up (we call it support), and so on. The same tools and approaches are used in analyzing and trading all the other markets.

In stocks, the charts are analyzed using the same candlesticks, indicators, and fundamental analysis. The same happens in the cryptocurrency market. When there is high-impact news, the cryptocurrency markets will be very volatile. The same would happen in the ETF and binary options markets. If we decided to do individual guides for each of the markets that we have, we would not only end up with a humongous book that we would never finish reading; the content would also be repetitive because, for the last time, they all use the same concepts. Therefore, don't think that we have focused too much on forex and left the other markets out.

## DEFINITION OF FOREX TRADING

Have you ever exchanged some dollars or any currency for a different currency? For example, you had dollars, and you went to a forex bureau or a bank, and they gave you sterling pounds, Yen, or something else. Maybe you had some cryptocurrency in your online wallet, and you converted it into a currency that you could withdraw and spend physically. If you answered "yes" to any of these, then you have already participated in forex trading. When you took your money to the exchanger, they charged you a little amount then gave you the other currency that you wanted. This is the same thing that happens in the online forex trading market.

In online trading, however, there are a few differences.

- One, you do not exchange physical cash with anybody. Rather, the exchange happens on dedicated trading platforms that we shall discuss later.

- Two, when trading online, you can borrow money from your broker to purchase (or exchange) more currency than what your capital would allow you to.

- Third, you can make as many exchanges as you wish by just clicking a simple button while seated in your living room or cooling off at the beach.

- Finally, unlike when you exchange physical cash and make no profits (in fact, you make losses in terms of what the bureaus charge!), in forex trading, you are the one who will be making the profits. Sounds interesting, doesn't it?

From the explanation above, we can say that forex trading is a form of trading where the currency of one country is quoted against the currency of another. You will see a lot of these side-by-side quotes once we start trading. When exchanging the US dollar with the Euro, we write it as EURUSD. If someone said the price of EURUSD was 1.505, they are simply saying that 1 Euro is equivalent to 1.505 US dollars. Similarly, if they say the price of GBPJPY is 135.10, then it means 1 Euro is equivalent to 135.10 Japanese Yen.

The forex market is interesting because it has no centralized exchange like futures and stocks. We can say that the DAX 30 is based at the Frankfurt Stock Exchange, and the S&P 500 is based in New York, but the forex market has no central place. Rather, it uses a method known as Over the Counter, OTC, which means it is not executed in any regulated environment. The aim of this huge market is to allow a quick and easy channel for countries, governments, central banks, businesses, and other international traders to convert currencies and do business with other nations across the globe.

As you can see, the forex market was not made just so people could trade. Rather, it is meant for big players who need to exchange currencies from time to time. Small-scale traders like us take advantage of the changes in currency rates to make profits by taking views on the direction of the exchange rates. All we need to do is predict whether the exchange rate of a certain quote will increase or decrease, then stand by and watch. Back to the EUR-USD, if the current price is

1.505, and from our analysis, we think the Euro will lose value against the dollar, we use the dollar to buy some Euros. In the market, we call this selling. If the price starts going lower than 1.505, we start making profits, the further it deviates from this figure. On the other hand, if the price starts getting higher than 1.505, then we start making losses.

Conversely, if we anticipate the Euro to gain value against the dollar, we will use the Euro to buy some dollars. This is called buying. If the price starts increasing beyond 1.505, we are going to start making profits, and the higher it goes, the more we make. If our analysis was wrong and the price began getting lower, then we will start making losses, and the lower it goes, the more we lose.

## MAIN PARTICIPANTS IN THE FOREX MARKET

Now that you have a clear understanding of what forex trading entails, let us look at the participants. These are the parties responsible for the changes in price every microsecond.

- **The first group of market participants is known as market makers.** In this group, we have international banks that have enough money to create changes in market prices. If they decide to buy a currency, they buy so much of it that its supply in the market reduces, causing it to gain in value. If they sell a currency, its supply in the market gets saturated, causing its value to depreciate. Probably you can see why they are called market makers.

- **The second group is known as multinationals.** It is composed of the biggest companies in the world. This is the group that does the actual exchange of one currency to another since they need different currencies to conduct business with other international firms. In addition to forex, they are also popular in stock trading and the futures market.

- **The third group is known as the speculators.** They utilize the market differently from the multinationals and market makers since their aim is to predict the direction of the market. They make their money by "betting" on possible price directions. In this group, you will find hedge funds, commercial banks, and commodity trading advisors, among others.

- **The fourth group consists of central banks from all over the world.** They are responsible for keeping the economies of their countries stable by regulating their currencies. To achieve this, they manage the way that their currencies are being traded. If they realize there is too much supply of it, they buy it to create demand, thus causing the value to increase. Similarly, if they realize that their currency is being used for speculation, which they hate, they move in to manipulate the market so as to keep the value stable.

- **The final group is known as retailers.** This is where individuals like us, and small-scale trading firms, are classified. We have no ability to manipulate the market, so all we do is predict the movement of price and make profits from it. In a way, we are small-scale speculators. This is the riskiest group since it has no power over the market and is, therefore, prone to sudden market movements caused by the big players. In fact, the big players are known to "hunt" our money when we are trading.

## OUR ROLE AS RETAIL TRADERS

Despite being ranked at the lower end of the trading hierarchy, retail traders are so numerous that collectively, they can move the market. The problem is that since there are too many of us, and each one of us understands the market differently, we cannot pile our resources together and move the prices. In short, some of us will be buying, as others sell. Others will be waiting as others are trading. At times, when we are going in, others are exiting. In the long run, we are found all over the place without order.

The above phenomenon makes us the prey of all the big players. Since they have the privilege of being able to move prices, they move prices against us and take our money. Unlike retailers, the big players have more market information, such as where retailers have placed the most trades. If they realize that the trades in that zone are "buy" orders, they execute large "sell" orders, and the retailers end up making losses.

While this might appear like something bad, if you can crack the way the big players see the market, then you can make profits when they make their moves. This is one of the reasons you need quality day trading information, and that is exactly what this book was made for. The strategies that we are going to be studying enable us to know when the price is likely to go higher, go lower, stagnate, and also when to keep off the markets.

We are going to use the same tools that the big players use and try to think as they do. This is called market analysis. In so doing, you will be able to predict when the big boys are about to make a big move that will move prices significantly. In doing so, while uninformed traders will be making losses, you will be flowing with the majority and will be making consistent profits as a day trader.

# CHAPTER 3

# THE FOUR MAJOR TRADING STYLES

Inside the world of trading, there has been a never-ending debate on whether short-term or long-term trading is the best. Short-term trading, also known as active trading, involves trading for minimal periods of time, ranging from seconds to a maximum of one day. Under this type of trading, we have scalping and day trading. Long-term trading, also known as buy-and-hold trading, involves trading for extended periods of time, ranging from a few days to months and even years. Under this category, we have swing trading and position trading. Traders in both categories claim their style is the best, and they give supporting reasons.

Let us look at the four major trading styles below and later explain why we settled on day trading.

## ACTIVE TRADING STYLES

### Scalping

The scalping style of trading is the quickest strategy that active traders use. When scalping, a person enters a trade and exits it within seconds or a few minutes. In short, they aim to take advantage of the slightest changes in prices and leave without allowing the risk of time to occur. This style is very popular in binary options and forex markets.

Due to the fast entry and exit times, scalpers make tiny profits. As such, they might need to trade numerous times in a day to achieve any targets or to make enough money. They also prefer very volatile markets with high liquidity since one needs sudden huge price movements to succeed in scalping.

### Day trading

The second type of active trading is day trading. This is a type of trade that is opened and closed on the same day; that is, it does not stay overnight. Day trading is the most popular and best-known trading style. Market makers and retail traders are known to prefer this method above the rest.

Unlike scalpers, day traders take more time with their trades, and they can manage them throughout the day. This style of trading is slower and takes advantage of intra-day price movements, which are moderate, although, during major economic events, the fluctuation of prices can be frantic.

## BUY-AND-HOLD TRADING STYLES

### Swing Trading

Swing trading is the most common strategy in buy-and-hold trading. Here, a trader identifies a trade opportunity, and they hold it for several days before closing it. Their aim is to catch and take advantage of huge price movements, unlike scalpers and day traders. Swing trading requires more experience and patience compared to any form of active trading.

In this trading style, the trader only checks their charts a few times a day. Once a trade has been opened, they only need to check in a few times, maybe twice, to see how their trades are performing. Again, the analysis required for swing trading is more demanding since one has to be able to foresee when a new move is about to occur as well as when it is expected to end.

### Position/Trend Trading

The second style of buy-and-hold trading is known as position or trend trading. In it, trades are executed and left to run for weeks, months, or years. The traders use larger timeframes in analyzing their charts to find long-term price directions. Position traders do not like high price fluctuations but a price that moves slowly and gradually toward their direction.

Position trading is mostly used by parties that have huge amounts of money, such as speculators and hedge funds.

## ADVANTAGES OF DAY TRADING

Our book title already specified that we are going to be exploring day trading. As such, any trades that you will open, whether in cryptocurrency, forex, binary options, options, ETFs, or futures, will be closed on the same day. I have been trading for well over a decade, and I had to try all four trading styles before settling on day trading. My conclusion was that scalping was too tiresome and risky, not to mention the emotional overload after placing several-second trades. Swing and position trading, on the other hand, was too boring for an impatient person like me who had to pay his bills from trading only.

Here are some of the reasons that I chose to go for day trading:

### 1. Ease of Getting Started

Day trading only requires a person to have the skills, a computer or smartphone, some little money, and a comfortable workstation. Getting the skills is as easy as finding a mentor who has been in the industry for some time (like you did by purchasing this book) and let them show you the profitable methods. You can also do it through practice and experience by reading tons of books and watching videos. However, this can be time-consuming and expensive since most of the information out there is too vague.

Second, since the trade positions held by a day trader are small, you do not need a lot of money to get started. Swing and position trading aims at riding huge price movements, which also come with the burden of sourcing for enough capital. With day trading, though, all you need is a few dollars, and you will be on your way to earning from trading.

## 2. Fewer Risks

The second advantage of day trading is that there are fewer risks involved. First, due to the short time required for holding positions, one is advised to risk only a small percentage of their account. In the event that losses occur, only a small amount is lost. Second, in day trading, you can open several positions within a day. As such, if some of the positions become losers, they can be closed and the profitable ones left to run. On the contrary, swing and position traders usually have very few trade opportunities. Therefore, when the trades turn into losers, they have no winning trades to cover the loss.

## 3. Daily Profits

How does it feel to end every day with your salary already paid? This is possible with day trading. Since all trades need to be closed by the end of the day, you will know how much you made or lost before going to bed. Day traders, therefore, have more peace of mind compared to long-term traders who might need to wait for days or months before knowing the fate of their trades.

## 4. More Opportunities

Once we start analyzing the charts, you will understand this better. Traders use what we call "timeframes" to analyze their charts. Scalpers use the least timeframes, which might be as low as 1 minute up to 5 minutes. Therefore, in a day, they can find tens or hundreds of opportunities. Day traders use 15-minute charts for up to 1 hour, meaning they get tens of opportunities. When it comes to the larger timeframes, such as daily, weekly, and monthly, trading opportunities might be fewer.

## 5. Fewer Transaction Costs

In the next chapter, you will learn that brokers charge a tiny amount of money for providing traders with market data and trading platforms. Whenever you make a trade, a little amount is charged. You will notice that some brokers charge an extra amount for trades that stay overnight. As such, a trade that runs for many days will be charged something daily. In the long run, the amount might accumulate and reduce one's profits or capital. Day traders, however, are not charged since they do not have sleepover trades.

## 6. Familiarity with the Markets

The last advantage of day trading is that due to spending a lot of time on the charts, the learner familiarizes themself with the movements of prices in the markets. In short, they get to understand the individual instruments that they are trading. I have found this to be true since I know how some stocks and currencies behave when the markets open, before important news releases and before prices start to change. All these have helped to increase my earnings and reduce my losses.

## DISADVANTAGES OF DAY TRADING

I like to be honest about everything. In light of this, let me reveal that while day trading might appear to be the perfect trading style, it has disadvantages of its own.

Let us look at them.

### 1. Higher Chances of Making Losses

Day trading can be very risky, especially for unskilled or uninformed traders. Since we make numerous trades within a day, if all of them or a majority of them were losers, it would cause significant harm to your account. Do not worry, though, because this book is meant to make you informed, so you can remain on the profitable side.

### 2. Tedious

Trading is a very interesting profession since you get to sit down, analyze charts, and watch as your money grows. However, when it is overdone, it can be tedious, just like anything else. Every trade requires proper analysis; so, the more trades that you make, the more likely you are to burn out. This can be avoided by setting specific times for trading and having a few instruments to analyze.

### 3. Price Fluctuations

The prices of all financial instruments change every microsecond. The rate of change might differ across markets. For example, stocks fluctuate less than currencies. The rate of change becomes more noticeable as one uses lower timeframes to do their analysis. That said, a day trader can be surprised by sudden price fluctuations due to unexpected economic events, and this might lead to losses. On the other hand, swing and position traders are less affected by changes in prices because they use larger timeframes, which fluctuate less.

As we have seen, traders have four trading styles where they can choose from. This can be determined by many factors. In our case, we have decided to go for day trading since the aim of this guide is to help you make a living out of online trading. Day trading is the only style in which you can set daily targets and know how much you will be earning in a month. In addition, it provides you with the chance to recover your losses since it provides tens of opportunities every day. Concisely, if you make losses today, you will still have more opportunities to recover them tomorrow. Swing trading provides fewer opportunities, and this might not be the most suitable trading style to achieve continuous cash flow.

# CHAPTER 4

## BASIC REQUIREMENTS FOR DAY TRADING

If there is something that I would never get tired of specifying, it is the fact that online trading should be respected as a professional career. You will come across people who trade as a hobby or just for fun, but they have their own reasons. When talking about day trading for a living, we are talking about the person who perceives trading as their sole source of income. That said, a serious trader should possess the skills and necessary tools to be successful in this art.

Let us take a mechanic for our example. The first things a person needs to become a mechanic are will and passion. No one should go into a profession for any reason other than self-motivation and passion. Second, they need to get the skills and knowledge required to take a car apart, troubleshoot problems, and satisfy the needs of their clients so they can be guaranteed to pay. Third, they need the tools to use in servicing, repairing, and upgrading motor vehicles. With these three requirements met, their chances of being successful mechanics are way above average.

Similarly, online day trading has requirements of its own. Make sure you possess the following arsenal before venturing into trading.

## 1. Mindset

I do not know why you decided to give online trading a try. However, I hope that you have a solid reason because this is going to be a very demanding journey. If you can recall what I said at the beginning, online trading is not easy. You will have to put in hundreds of practice hours, intense research, and unending education. Therefore, the first tool that you require as a day trader is the proper mindset.

One aspect that you should embrace is that trading is not a get-rich-quick scheme. You will have to build experience and practice a lot before you can start making money like the big players who probably inspired you to pursue this interesting career.

Second, and very importantly, be ready to fail numerous times before you finally crack it. Trading is like an investment game where tricks of all manners will be put into use. You will make mistakes that will lead to losses, but with time, you will understand the rules of the game ad that is where your success will begin. In short, you need a fighting mindset.

## 2. Education

I believe you already have the first requirement, judging by how far you came in search of this knowledge. You are now onto the second requirement, which is education. A trader needs to know how to trade. This book is an example of the education that you need. There is no point in elaborating this point any further.

## 3. A Computer

You can use several devices to learn to trade, as well as to do trading, such as computers, smartphones, tablets, and so on. Personally, I would recommend a computer because of the analysis part. You will be opening charts of the trading instruments that have a lot of graphical details. In this case, a big display will allow you to see even the smallest details clearly. In addition, mobile versions of the trading platforms are simplified, meaning some of the tools might be missing.

A simple computer will do. It only needs to have a big display of about 21 inches. I started out with a 17-inch monitor, and it worked well for me. However, when I graduated to a bigger screen, I could see more of the charts, and it simplified my analysis. Here is a summary of the minimum specifications that your computer should have:

- Windows, Mac, or Linux operating system

- Core 2 duo processor and above

- Minimum 40GB of hard disk capacity

- 2GB of RAM

**Note:** These are only my recommendations. You can use a computer with different (lower) specifications, and it might just work out well. Second, you can use two monitors such that one screen will be used for the analysis, and the other one can be used for placing the orders. This is optional.

## 4. Stable Internet Connection

This is where you do not have too many options. Internet connection quality is very important in online trading as it is the channel through which you receive market data, place trades, and connect with your broker. Therefore, make sure your internet is fast and reliable. Any disconnection or delay can give wrong charting information or even lead to losses during trading.

### 5. A Broker

A broker is a party that will give you a trading platform, allows you to deposit and withdraw money, and also provide you with trading market data. There are thousands of online trading brokers today. In this area, too, you need the best broker. They must be genuine, trustworthy, reliable, and accessible.

### 6. Charting Software

Charting Software is also known as a trading platform. This is the application where analysis is done, and orders are executed, as well as managed. There are different types of charting software that you can use. We shall look at the installation of some main ones before delving into the strategies.

### 7. A Trading Plan

A trading plan is also known as a strategy. This is one of the most important tools in your trading arsenal. The trading plan acts as a guide in helping a trader to make proper trading decisions. It can be summarized as a personal trading constitution, as it contains the rules that govern everything that a trader does in their line of work. This will also be discussed toward the end of the guide.

### 8. A Trading Account

You will need a good trading account. This is the central point from where you will access the trading platform, connect with your broker, deposit and withdraw your funds, and so on. You need an email address, a phone number, and a few documents, such as a scan of your ID, a recent bank statement, and a utility bill containing your address.

Before creating a real account that will ask for the mentioned documents, you can open a demo trading ac-

count. This is a trading account used for practice purposes. You are provided with free money, although you
cannot withdraw it. A demo account works like a real
trading account, only that you do not need to deposit
your own funds. Most brokers provide demo accounts
for free. We shall go through the steps of opening a
trading account when installing the trading platforms.

## 9. A working station

Finally, now that you have committed to becoming
a day trader, it is time to set up an office. First of all,
your computer needs a table or desk. Next, you need
a comfortable ergonomic chair since you will be seated throughout your working sessions. It is advisable to
make the workstation as comfortable as possible as
this influence might your mood. A neat, well-lit workstation will not only motivate you to work but also make
the working day enjoyable. Add some colored lighting,
fluffy carpets, polished furniture, soothing music, or
just anything that you feel will enhance your working
environment.

With all the above tools, you will be armed, ready to experience the world of online trading. Please remember
that you can substitute any of these tools with something different for your convenience. However, if you
can find them exactly as I have outlined them or better,
you will have a smooth time learning and eventually
working as a day trader.

# CHAPTER 5
## TERMINOLOGY

Online trading has unique phrases and brief terms that are commonly used in communicating by traders. These words are very specific to this profession that they may appear as jargon to non-traders or traders who have not taken their time in learning them. It can be both risky and unprofessional to start trading without getting to understand the meaning of the terms that are commonly used terms in any field.

You do not have to memorize them. I would recommend that you understand what they mean, as this will help you internalize them better. As we go along the day trading journey, we shall be using them, so by the end of it, their meanings will be at your fingertips. Again, these terms are shared across any type of trading that you might look into.

### ARBITRAGE

This is a method of trading where one takes advantage of price differences between two financial instruments. In stocks, for example, a share might be selling for $29 in one market and $32 in another. A trader can buy the share in the cheap market then sell it immediately in the secondary market to make a profit of the difference ($3).

## ASK PRICE

This is also known as the "offer price." It refers to the price or value at which a seller is willing to accept for an instrument. If you place a EUR-USD trade at 1.234, that is your ask price.

## ASSET

An asset refers to the instrument that is being traded. If a trader is focusing on stocks, their assets are all the shares of companies that they can trade. In crypto trading, Bitcoin and all the other cryptos are the assets.

## AT THE MONEY

This is also known as "break-even." It happens when, at the end of a trade, or during the closure of a particular trade, the value of the asset being traded is the same as the asking price (opening price). Usually, at break-even, the trader neither makes a profit nor a loss.

## BASE CURRENCY/COUNTER CURRENCY

In forex, cryptocurrency, and binary options trading, the assets are expressed as currency A/currency B. Examples are EURUSD, BTCUSD. The currency on the left is known as the "base currency," while the one on the right is called the "counter currency."

## BEAR MARKET

A bear market is a term used to define a downward movement of the price or value of an asset. This is when traders open "Sell" trades.

## BID PRICE

This is the price or value that a buyer is willing to pay for the acquisition of a trading asset. When placing a trade, the ask price is quoted, as well as the bid price. There is usually a small difference between the two, which the broker keeps as profit.

## BONUS

A bonus is any type of incentive or gift that a broker might offer their clients. It can also be referred to as a promotion. Once you start trading, you will see brokers offering all types of bonuses to lure or appreciate their clients.

## BOUNDARY

This term is common in binary options. It refers to the time allowed before an asset being traded expires. In short, if you predict that the value of a stock will go higher within 10 minutes, this time is known as the boundary.

## BULL MARKET

A bull market is the opposite of a bear market. It is the moment when the value or price of a market seems to be going up. During bullish markets, traders will mostly be placing "Buy" trades.

## COMMODITY

A commodity is a type of trading asset that involves raw materials such as metals (silver, gold, copper, etc.), natural fuels (oil and gas), and major agricultural products, such as livestock, cocoa, and coffee.

## CURRENT RATE

This is the present value or price of an asset.

## EARLY CLOSURE

Just like the phrase sounds, it refers to the ability to exit a running trade immediately without delay.

## EXPIRY

This is the date or time when an open trade is scheduled to be closed. It is at this point that the results of trades are determined.

## EQUITY

Equity is the alternative name for investment, deposit, or capital that is available in a trading account.

## GAP

A gap is a significant difference between two quotes; it is usually unrecorded on the trading charts. It can be explained as a "space" where the values of an asset were not captured. Gaps are common during sudden market movements or during weekends and public holidays when the markets are closed.

## INDEX

An index (plural "indices") is a method of grouping several assets or securities under one group, so their performance can be measured as one unit. A good example is the FTSE, which is the measure of the top 100 capitalized firms at the London Stock Exchange.

## IN THE MONEY

This means that a trade is making profits, or it has closed at a profit.

## LEVERAGE

Leverage is one of the most crucial terms used in trading. It is a feature provided by brokers where a trader can "borrow" some money from them to place bigger trades than their actual capital can allow. It is expressed in ratios such as 1:50, meaning for each dollar that a trader holds, they can "borrow" fifty times more from the broker to place bigger trades that can offer bigger returns. Leverage is as risky as it is interesting since it can magnify losses.

## MARGIN

Margin is the amount of money that is required to sustain an open trade. If a trade makes losses, it uses more margin and causes a reduction in the available equity. When the equity gets exhausted, the open trade or trades are terminated.

## MARKET PRICE

The market price refers to the real value of an asset as provided from the main market at a specific time.

## ORDER

An order is a transaction that a trader places. In short, when you open a buy or sell order, you have placed an order. Call and Put are also examples of orders in options trading.

There are two main types of orders:

- **Opening orders**

Opening orders are the actions intended to execute (open) a new trade. There are different types of opening orders.

  » *Market Order:* An "open" market order means that when the trader presses the button to enter a trade, it happens immediately at the current market value.

  » *Buy-Stop:* A Buy-Stop order happens when a trader analyzes the market and concludes that, after the price or value reaches a certain point in the future, it will go higher. Therefore, they place a pending order at the chosen point. Then when the market reaches it, a "buy" order is automatically opened.

  » *Sell-Stop:* A Sell-Stop order is the opposite of a Buy-Stop order. The trader places a pending order in a future position; then, when the market value hits it, a "Sell" order is automatically opened.

» **Buy-Limit:** A Buy-Limit order happens when a trader analyzes their charts and concludes that when the market falls to a certain point in the future, it will stop falling and start going up. Therefore, they place a pending, and when the market reaches it, a "Buy" order is automatically opened.

» **Sell-Limit:** A Sell-Limit order is the opposite of a Buy-Limit. However, this time, the trader has concluded that when the market value reaches a certain level in the future, it will stop rising and start trading lower. As such, they place a pending order, and when the market touches it, a "Sell" order is automatically opened.

• **Closing orders**

Closing orders are the actions intended to close active (running) trades. There are four types of closing orders. They are:

» **Market Order:** A "Close" market order means that when the trader presses the button to exit a trader, it is executed immediately.

» **Take-Profit:** A Take-Profit order is used to automatically close a trade that is in profit. The trader first opens a trade and then sets a Take-Profit level. When the profitable trade gets to the pre-set level, it automatically closes the trade and keeps the profits.

» **Stop-Loss:** A Stop-Loss order is used to automatically close a losing trade. The trader first initiates a trade and then places a Stop-Loss level in the future. If the losing trade gets to that level, it automatically closes the trade and stops further losses.

» **Trailing Stop:** A Trailing Stop order is an automatic type of order that seeks to book and protect a trader's profits. As such, it only works for trades that are already on the profit side. To set it, a trade decides on a number of pips or points, after which the Trailing Stop is to be launched. Let's say you have a trade that is already 30 pips in profit. You can set a 10-pip Trailing Stop, meaning that after the trade has made 20 pips of profit, it will place a stop-loss order at 10 pips of profit. After another 10 pips of profit (40 pips), it will automatically move the stop-loss at 20 pips. If the market reverses and hits the stop-loss, the trade is closed, and the profits are kept.

## OUT OF THE MONEY

This means that an active trade is on the losing side, or a particular trade has been closed at a loss.

## PIP

A "pip" the acronym for "point in percentage" is mostly applied in the forex market. It is the measure, in points, of the distance that the value of an asset moves. For instance, if the rate of the USDJPY moves from 135.60 to 135.40, then we say it has moved 20 pips down.

## SLIPPAGE

Slippage is an occurrence that happens during the opening and/or closing of a trade where, due to the fast movement of the market, the resulting value differs from the intended one. For example, you want to place a gold versus US dollar trade (XAUUSD) when the market price is 1500. After you press the button to open the order, there is a sharp, sudden movement in price, and the order gets placed at price 1502. In this case, we say there has been a slippage of 2 points or pips.

## SPREAD

The spread is the difference between the ask price and the bid price. It is the amount, in pips, that a broker charges for each trade. So, if the market price of an instrument is 120 and the broker provides an ask price of 121 of which you agree to buy it at 122, then the spread in that trade is (122-121) = 1 pip.

## SWAP

A swap is a charge that occurs when one currency is exchanged for another. It is common in the forex market and usually happens at midnight. If the value of the currency that you have bought has gained against the value of the currency that you are selling, then you are paid a little sum by the broker. If the opposite occurs, then you pay the broker a little sum.

## QUOTE

A quote, mostly used in currency trading, is the expression of the base currency versus the counter currency. As such, XAUUSD, GBPUSD, and EURUSD are all examples of quotes.

Speaking the language of online trading is the first step toward being successful. You need to be conversant with what the most important terms in the industry mean. This way, your study and practice will be flawless. The above list of common terminology used in trading is not conclusive; there are countless more. However, they are enough to help you get started. As your time spent in day trading increases, you will come across thousands of other words that we use. Please refer to this chapter any time you find unclear words in your trading journey.

# CHAPTER 6
## TRADING PLATFORMS

Day traders have a variety of trading platforms to choose from. A trading platform is a program or software that a trader uses to access market data, conduct their analysis, and place trades. There are tens of available platforms in the market. Recently, due to the growth of the trading industry, more options have been introduced, and competition has become stiff. At the end of the day, it is up to the trader to decide on the platform or platforms to use.

## PLATFORMS YOU COULD USE

In this section, we are going to discuss some of the most popular platforms available in the market. You can consider the features we are going to discuss as a filter to help you in choosing your best platform. All the same, I will recommend the one platform that I have used all my life.

### MetaTrader 4 (MT4)

MT4 is one of the oldest trading platforms in the industry. It is one of the programs that led to the growth of retail traders as it enabled them to access the market. Traders find it highly reliable and easy to use, making it the most popular trading platform in use for decades now. I personally prefer it over any other platform for several reasons such as:

- It is highly stable.

- It supports a lot of indicators, trading instruments, and robots.

- It can work on all mobile and computer operating systems.

- It is available in almost all brokerage companies.

- It is free.

### MetaTrader 5 (MT5)

Just like the names suggest, MT4 and MT5 are related since they are made by the same company (Metaquotes). Their major difference is that the MT5 platform is more advanced and includes more features than the MT4. For instance, the MT5 is even more stable. It is faster, holds more robots and indicators, and also comes with more trading instruments.

It is advisable that even if you start out with MT4, you should gradually transition to MT5 as the older platform may stop being used in the future. We are going to base our learning on this newer trading platform. You can also use the MT4 as they operate the same way.

### Ninja Trader

The Ninja Trader platform is quite young compared to the MT4. It came into the market in 2004. All the same, some traders prefer it over the MT4. While the MT4 is mostly suitable for trading currencies (forex and cryptocurrency), the Ninja Trader readily supports forex, stock, and futures trading. In addition to this, the platform offers trade simulation, automated strategy development, and advanced charting tools and abilities. Some disadvantages of the Ninja Trader that keep the MT4 in the lead include:

- Users must buy a license or lease the platform to be able to execute trades.

- Plug-ins like indicators and robots are not free.

- It is not a market data provider, so traders must connect to a data provider like Kinetick or Google.

### cTrader

The cTrader software comes third after the Metaquotes platforms and Ninja Trader. It has been displaying stiff competition in recent years, and many brokers have been taking it up. Some of the features that make it highly competitive include fast trade execution, cheaper costs of trades, vast device support, and advanced charting capabilities. However, unlike the other platforms, it does not support Windows Phone OS.

### ProRealTime

ProRealTime is a web-based platform (it does not need to be installed on a computer) as it is backed up on the cloud network of the company. It uses a unique coding language (ProRealCode) to create market analyzing tools. While this feature makes it unique, it also means there are fewer tools available online. Another disadvantage is that users must pay to use the platform and access real-time data.

### eSignal

eSignal might not be the most popular trading platform, but it is a favorite tool for advanced traders who prefer to customize their own trading approaches. Once a trader learns the supported coding language, they can create their own indicators, trading strategies, and other analytic tools. In addition, eSignal allows a trader to view over 500 trading instruments at a go.

On the downside, traders must pay annual or monthly fees to gain access to market feed. Second, the platform is not common in most brokerage companies.

Remember, it is up to you as the trader to decide on the type of trading platform to use. In our case, though, we are going to use the MT5 as it is user-friendly and contains all the necessary tools, instruments, and features that a trader needs.

## INSTALLING THE TRADING PLATFORM

The trading platforms are available on the brokers' websites. You need to sign up with a broker of your choice before accessing any trading platform. Once registered, the broker will provide you with a list of all the trading platforms that they support for you to choose from. The installation process is quite simple and usually requires filling in some personal details and other information that will be provided by the broker.

In our case, we shall be using the MT5, which is very similar to the MT4 platform. The MT5 is very easy to install. To make it even better, we can use the platform for learning purposes without signing up with any broker. However, this will only be a demo account. To access the MT5, head over to the Metaquotes website, and download the MT5. I recommend this method because you will not have to undergo the long process of applying for an account. You can do this when you are ready to use a live account.

Once you have downloaded the MT5 file to your computer, run it and make sure your internet is active. When the installation is complete, a window like the one below should open up.

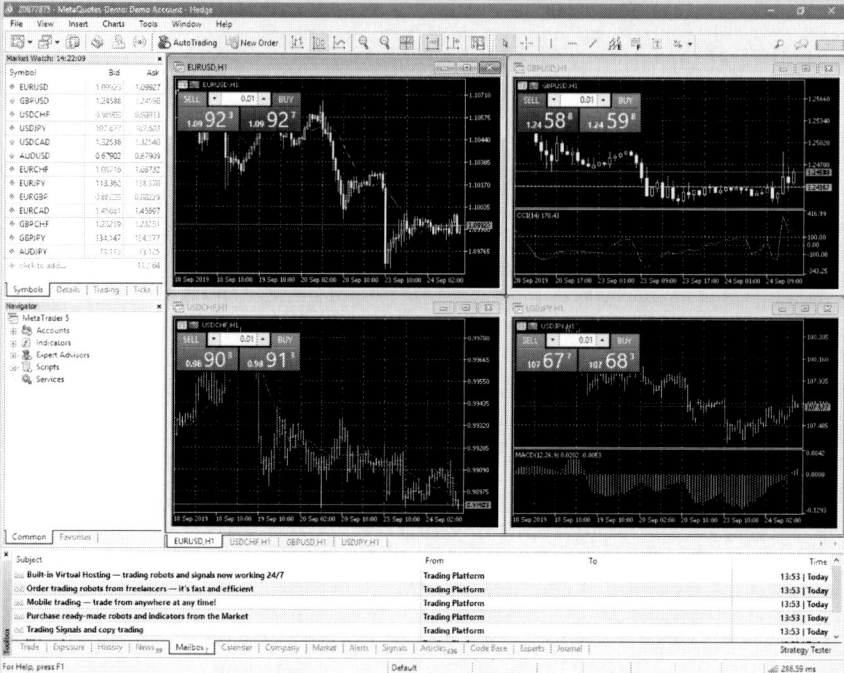

*The MT5 platform.* **Source**: *Metaquotes MT5*

If you successfully get to this point, then you are ready to start your journey to successful day trading.

**Note:** Let me remind you that the MT5 platform can be used to trade stocks, futures, and forex (including cryptocurrency). Therefore, even though we shall be using a forex chart for the lessons, remember that the appearance, operation, and analysis are the same in the other markets. As such, you can apply the lessons that you will get here to trade in any of the other markets.

## TYPES OF CHARTS ON MT5

Now that you have the trading platform ready, let us look at the types of charts that you can use. The four windows with a lot of graphics that you can see above are known as charts. Let us look at the three types of charts that we can use for analyzing the market.

## Line Chart

To activate a line chart, you need to first select one of the charts in the open windows. In my case, I have chosen the EURUSD chart. You can see the title of the charts on the top-right corners. Once you have chosen your chart, click on the "Line chart" icon at the top of your MT5.

You should end up with a chart like this one:

*A line chart*

You will see a green line in the resulting chart. That line is called an indicator. We shall look at them later, but for now, you need to get rid of them. To do so:

- Right-click inside the EURUSD chart

- Go to the "Indicator List" option and click it

- You will see "Moving Average." Click it and press "Delete."

Your line chart will now be plain.

So, what you are now looking at is called a line chart. This is a simple graphic that represents the movement of prices. When it is sloping upward, it means the price was increasing, and when it slopes downward, it means the price was decreasing.

### *Bar Chart*

To activate a bar chart, you need to click on the "Bar chart" tool at the top of your MT5.

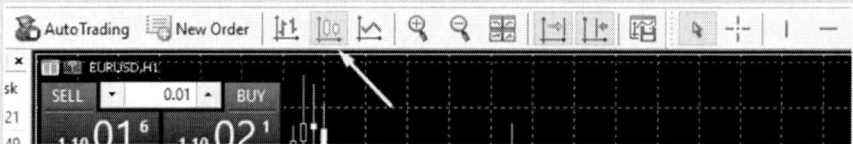

You should end up with a chart like this one:

What you are looking at is right now is a bar chart. Unlike a line chart, the bar chart has more details. It shows the opening and closing of prices. You will see that there are vertical lines with tiny horizontal lines on either side. They are called "hashes." The hashes on the left show the opening prices, while those on the right show the closing prices. The top of the bars represents the highest point that price went, while the bottom part shows the lowest point that price touched.

A single bar represents time. Inside the charts, next to the name of the currency pair, you can see the label "H1," which means that each bar in the chart takes 1 hour to form. You can change the timeframe, and see the formation of bars for every 1, 5, 15, 30, 60 minutes up to 1 month by choosing any of the times shown in this frame:

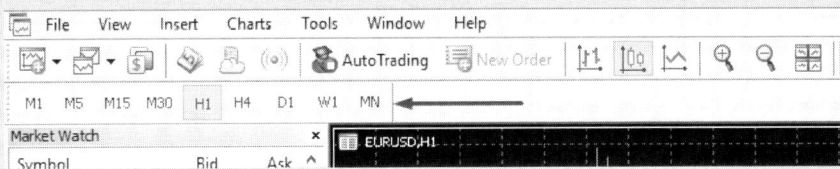

Bar charts are also known as OHLC charts where 'O' stands for the opening price, 'H' for the highest point that price went, 'L' for the lowest point, and 'C' for the closing price of the bar.

### Candlestick Charts

Candlestick charts are the most interesting charts. They use bars that look like candles with wicks to show the performance of price. Just like bar charts, they also show the open and closing prices, as well as the highs and lows of prices. However, they look different in that they have wider bodies and single lines on either side called 'wicks.' Candlestick bars are also colored to represent prices going up or down within a selected timeframe.

To activate a candlestick bar, click the "candlesticks" icon next to where you found the line and bar chart icons.

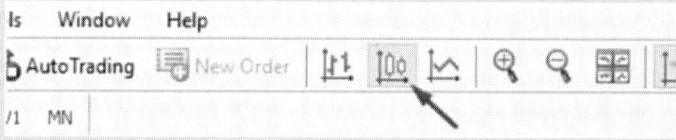

You should end up with a chart like the one below:

*A candlestick chart*

As you can see from the chart, some bars have white bodies and green wicks. These ones show that within that time (1 hour), the price of the EUR-USD went down. The price opened at the top of the white body and closed on the opposite end of the white body. The green wicks on top of the white body show the highest point that the price reached before coming down, while the ones on the opposite side show the lowest point that the price reached before going up again. These bars are also known as "bearish candles."

The other candles have black bodies and green wicks. These candles showed when the price went up. In short, during that hour, the rate of the EUR-USD went higher. The wicks on the upper side show the highest point that price went before falling, while the wicks on the lower side show the lowest point that price went before rising again. These candles are also known as "bullish candles."

You can customize the colors of the candles as you wish. In most cases, bearish candles are filled with red color, while bullish ones are filled with green. However, the colors have no effect on one's trading; they only help one to see price behavior more clearly.

In our trading journey, we shall be using candlestick charts, just like the majority of traders do. Here are a few reasons for this decision:

- First, due to their shapes and color, it is very easy to interpret what price is doing. A red bar will instantly tell you that the price went lower within a certain time.

- Second, and very importantly for traders, candlesticks form patterns that we can use to interpret and predict the market. There are hundreds of patterns formed by candlesticks as the market moves, and by understanding them, one can become a successful trader. We shall look at the most important patterns in the next chapter.

Before this chapter, you probably heard the word "charting" and wondered what it meant. Hopefully, now, you know what charts are in the trading industry. With that knowledge in mind, it is time to put it to work by discussing market analysis.

# CHAPTER 7

## MARKET ANALYSIS

After all the theories and information that you have been reading, market analysis is where your actual trading journey starts. The analysis is the process by which traders study the charts and use the knowledge in making decisions about their trades. We say that market analysis is not part of trading; it is the whole essence of trading.

This is another controversial context in the trading industry because traders never seem to agree on which, between the two major types of market analysis, is best. There are actually three types of market analyses. However, only two of them are popular since the third is usually a personal method. So, what are these three types of chart analysis?

They are:

1.  Fundamental analysis

2. Technical analysis, and

3. Sentimental analysis

Let us look at what each one of them entails.

### FUNDAMENTAL ANALYSIS

Fundamental analysis is a type of market analysis that tries to derive the underlying value of a financial instrument or asset by studying and assessing economic data. In this approach, the traders do not need to look at the charts to determine the future of the market. Rather, they seek all the relevant data about the instruments they are trading and then use the information to make their trades. Some of the economic data that traders look at closely include inflation, employment, GDP, exports, imports, interest rates, central banks' activities, and so on.

The objective of fundamentalists is to use economic reports as indicators to predict the overall conditions of the market. Out of this analysis, they hope to spot trading opportunities that promise high returns and minimum risk. In a nutshell, fundamentalist traders interpret present economic data and then use the information to decide whether an instrument is likely to gain or lose value in the future. For instance, they know that if a report comes out about Facebook launching a new product and the public is highly anticipative of it, the value of the Facebook share (stock) is likely to appreciate in the future. As such, they will buy stocks in anticipation of the growth in value.

Here are some of the economic data that fundamentalists focus on.

- **The economy**

The status of an economy directly affects the value of a country's currency, imports, exports, and other factors. If a country's economy is doing well, then its currency will grow stronger. Its exports will cost more, and the imports will be cheaper. For instance, when the price of oil increases, the value of all the currencies that produce and export the commodity will grow. Similarly, if the growth of an economy is reported to have dropped, the value of its currency and export commodities will decrease.

- **Political stability**

Political stability leads to increased confidence in the commodities or currencies of independent countries. On the other hand, political instability erodes investor confidence, leading to less investment and deterioration of economic performance. A good example was in 2018 when Facebook was entangled in the Cambridge Analytical scandal, where it was accused of interfering with the electoral process in Kenya, an East African country. On the first day of the report, Facebook shares lost close to $18 billion. By the time the scandal had stabilized, the company had lost over $134 billion. In this case, any trader that had sold the stock made a lot of money.

- **Government policies**

Government policies, such as interest rates, have significant effects on the general performance of currencies and commodities. When interest rates are increased, this curbs inflation and slows economic growth. Similarly, reducing interest rates stimulates economies by promoting investment. Other aspects, like fiscal policies, also affect the movement of the market. For example, high taxation slows economic performance and discourages business.

- **Observing market makers**

There are traders who wait for the big players in the market to make their moves; then they will jump in and flow with the tide. They base their decisions on the assumption that the big players have the ability to move the markets. If they can spot the big moves as they start, then they can reap big profits. Such traders will, therefore, place their focus on hedge funds, governments, central banks, and other huge financial institutions.

- **Reports and news events**

Do you remember 9/11? If so, then this point will be easy to understand. When the tragic news went live, the dollar plunged immediately. In about 5 days, the US economy had lost over $1.4 billion. In this case, anyone who had bought the EUR-USD would have made a lot of money. Similarly, any trader who had sold the USD-JPY would have made handsome profits as well.

Another event is when, in 2019, a Boeing 737 MAX crashed in Ethiopia a few months after a similar plane had crashed in Indonesia. Both flights killed all the passengers and crew. Controversy emerged that the plane model was unsafe. In just a few days, the shares of Boeing sunk by 12%, which is close to $27 billion from the market. A trader who had analyzed this event and sold the Boeing stocks would have made a lot of money from the decline in price.

Do you now understand how fundamental analysis works?

### Advantages of Fundamental Analysis

- First, since fundamentalists seek to predict the movement of the markets before they happen, they can easily explain why a movement occurred. This fact alone is enough to increase one's predictive ability and profits.

- Second, studying economic data can help a trader to know the long-term position of price. In short, they can place trades and know where to anticipate the market to reach in the future. This improves their confidence when they have active trades.

- Third, due to the amount of data that is collected and analyzed, a trader gains a better understanding of the markets. As such, they can predict the markets more accurately and reduce guesswork.

### *Disadvantages of Fundamental Analysis*

- The biggest downside of fundamental analysis is that it lacks definite timing. A trader might know that the price of a stock will decline in the future, but they have no specific time when the fall will start. This is very risky when trading.

- Second, due to the lack of proper timing, this approach is not suitable for short-term trading, such as day trading or scalping. However, there are some types of fundamentals that can be used for day trading.

- The third disadvantage is that collecting too much economic data can lead to information overload. When this happens, the trader is unable to process the information. In the long run, they might make wrong decisions that can lead to losses.

- The final disadvantage is that interpreting economic information might vary. One trader might believe that a market will ascend while another interprets the same data in the opposite direction. A wrong interpretation can lead to inaccurate analysis and losses.

## TECHNICAL ANALYSIS

Technical analysis is the approach of analyzing the market using the movements of prices in the past. This approach is usually said to be more of an art than it is a science since it mostly uses observation, as opposed to complex formulas and derivations. This time, unlike in fundamental analysis, the trader relies on the charts found in the trading platforms to make their decisions. They do not need to try and interpret economic data but read what the charts are saying.

The most important tool in technical analysis is price data. Different timeframes will display different information, but, all the same, price data must be used to make the trading decisions. Basically, technical analysis studies past and present actions of price and helps the trader to predict the future behavior of the market. The behavior of price is studied using tools like the candlestick, lines, and bar charts that we saw earlier. This approach will work best where the instrument being traded, be it a stock, index, commodity, currency, futures, or option, has enough liquidity and is not susceptible to external influences.

Technical analysis is based on three major assumptions:

- First, that price behavior supersedes all other information, such as economic data. Technical traders firmly believe that the present behavior of price contains all the information about the market. Also, any new information is captured and shown immediately. Concisely, they do not believe so much in the fundamental approach.

- Second, markets move in observable patterns. Technical traders assert that the market moves in patterns that can be observed and used to predict the future movement of prices. However, one has to be trained to observe the patterns when they form. The most-used observable pattern in trading is known as a 'trend.' A trend is a definite direction (up or down) that price seems to be following.

- Third, in the market, history will always be repeated. This assumption is closely related to the above point in that once a pattern has been observed, it can be expected to continue in a certain direction until the pattern has been completed. Repetition in price patterns can be seen in candlestick patterns, volume, chart formations, and momentum, to mention but a few.

## *Advantages of Technical Analysis*

- By using charts, it is possible to choose any timeframe and focus on analyzing the market for a specific time. This is very important in day trading because we need timeframes that are less than one day to conduct our studies of price.

- Charts are visual tools; therefore, they enable us to see trends. Trends show the overall direction that the price is moving. In short, from a chart, we can see whether a market is bullish or bearish before deciding to buy or sell an instrument.

- The timing feature in the charts helps day traders to plan their working hours. They can decide when to work, when to break, or when to close their trades since they do not have to be carried over past midnight. In fundamental analysis, a trader's trading time is determined by external factors, such as the time when important data will be released.

- Technical analysis is preferred by many traders because it allows for the automation of concepts. Programmers can create automatic tools known as indicators and expert advisors (robots) to help with analyzing the market as well as entering or exiting trades.

- The other advantage of technical analysis is that it easily highlights important zones in the market. For example, you can tell where the market is likely to make a U-turn by looking at the charts. You will read more about this under Support and Resistance.

- Finally, compared to fundamental analysis, technical analysis is less consuming as the trader does not have to pursue different channels of information so they can make their trades. In the latter, we only need to look at the charts.

## *Disadvantages of Technical Analysis*

- Charting is not as easy as it might sound. One reason is that different timeframes can give different signals. A 1-hour timeframe might predict a rising price, while the 15-minute chart shows a falling price. Such occurrences can be confusing.

- There is another issue that is closely related to the above point, known as analysis paralysis. This is where a trader overanalyzes their charts until they get too confused to make a confident decision.

- Third, due to the presence of thousands of automated indicators and robots, different traders might interpret the market differently. Automated systems may not necessarily work the same, thus the varying signals. This can also lead to confusion or wrong analysis.

- Finally, while technical analysts might ignore fundamentals, this approach might have significant influences on their analysis. During major news or events, the market might ignore any formations and patterns that have formed, leading to wrong analysis or losses.

## SENTIMENTAL ANALYSIS

Sentimental analysis is not as popular as the two other approaches, but still, it is used by some day traders. Unlike the other two, sentimental analysis is based on the trader's opinion and not on any external factors. In short, the trader will look at the market and provide personal opinions on whether the market is going up or down.

One of the methods used in the sentimental analysis is measuring the ratios between the buyers and the sellers. If the buyers (called 'bulls') are more, the trader is likely to place "buy" trades. On the other hand, if the sellers (called 'bears') appear to be in charge, then the trader is more likely to place "sell" trades.

The sentimental approach is the riskiest of the three. As such, traders usually use it together with any of the two major approaches.

## FUNDAMENTAL OR TECHNICAL ANALYSIS?

You are now part of this huge battle since you chose to become a trader!

Well, any seasoned trader will tell you that all three forms of analysis are very important in day trading. The three approaches should complement each other if a trader needs to increase their winning ratio. When one of them is ignored, the risks of making the wrong predictions increase.

Due to the above revelation, we are going to use all three methods. However, technical analysis will be the dominant one. I have chosen the technical approach because day trading needs sharper accuracy compared to position and swing trading. In addition, I find observation to be more revealing than just basing my decisions on verbal information. In my many years of trading, I have come to prove that, indeed, history repeats itself in the markets. You will also realize the same.

The tools found in charts, together with the historical behavior of price, will help us to understand and foretell the potential direction of the markets with significant accuracy. All the same, even as we focus on technical analysis, we shall also include a few important fundamentals and how to utilize them for better gains in day trading.

Next, we look at candlestick patterns.

# CHAPTER 8

## CANDLESTICK PATTERNS

The candlesticks that we are talking about are actually known in full as "Japanese Candlesticks." They were invented by a Japanese trader and later grew in popularity in the 90s. Since their importance was discovered, Japanese candlestick charts have become the most popular type of trading chart used today.

### ANATOMY OF CANDLESTICKS

Japanese candlesticks contain very important information about the market. A trader can read the market like an open book once they understand the anatomy of a candlestick. This is usually the first and very important step toward successful trading. You need to understand what the market or price is doing so you can make appropriate decisions. In this chapter, we are going to break down the candlesticks and understand what each shape and pattern tells us about the market.

Before we start, let me clarify that our bullish candles will have white bodies and black tips, while the bearish ones will have black bodies and black wicks. You can use any color of your preference by changing it in your MT5. To do so, right-click inside your chart window, click on "properties" then adjust the colors as you wish.

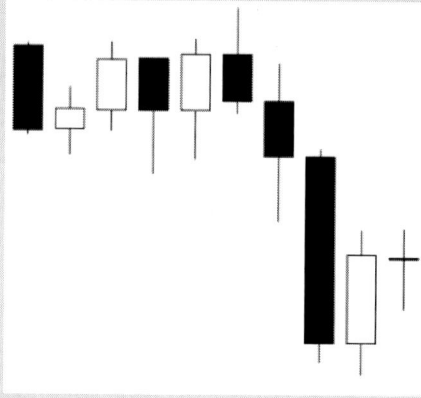

*Black candlesticks are bearish, and white candlesticks are bullish*

## Candlestick Bodies

When you look at your charts, you will realize that candlesticks come in different sizes. Some of them are very tiny, while some are huge. These sizes actually mean something!

The short bodies mean there was little buying or selling activity. The short white candlesticks mean that there was little buying activity. The short black candles mean there was little selling activity

On the other hand, long bodies mean there was a lot of buying or selling. Long white candlesticks mean there was a lot of buying activity, and the bulls were in control of the market. Similarly, the long black candlesticks mean there was a lot of selling activity, and the bears were in control. The longer the candlesticks are, the more buying or selling activity was happening in the market.

## Candlestick Wicks

The wicks on the candles also have very important information.

The wicks on the upper side of the candlesticks show that the bulls pushed prices high before sellers came in and pushed the price lower. Those on the lower side show that the sellers tried to take the price lower, but the bulls came in and pushed it higher. As a trader, you should always perceive the market as a battle where the bulls are always fighting against the sellers, as they seek to control the direction of the markets.

Long shadows on the upper side of a candle show that there was a lot of buying pressure, and the buyers were in control of the market for some time before the bears came in with more power and lowered the prices. Short shadows on the upper side show that there was no buying pressure, or the bulls were not interested in driving prices past that level.

In the same way, long shadows on the lower side of a candle show that there was a lot of selling pressure from the bears, but the bulls came in with more power, and they raised the prices. Short wicks on the lower side of a candle indicate low-selling pressure or lack of interest in further selling by the bears.

## THE MOST POWERFUL CANDLESTICK PATTERNS

Candlesticks are formed by price behavior, which is known as Price Action in trading. These charts can be used as standalone analysis tools or as confirmations for trading signals. Traders also add robots and indicators to candlestick charts to improve their accuracy.

At times, the markets will form interesting candlestick formations that have very important information. Price action traders are always on the lookout for these formations that we shall call "patterns." When these patterns occur, they tell us that the market is about to do something. An existing trend (price direction) can continue or reverse after a special candlestick pattern has formed.

Candlestick patterns can be formed by one or more candles in a sequence. At this level, we are going to look at patterns formed by single, double, and triple candlesticks.

### Single Candlestick Patterns

These patterns are made up of a single candlestick that has special anatomy. Here are some of the most important single-candlestick patterns.

### DOJI

A Doji is the simplest pattern to spot in your charts. It is formed when the price opens and closes at the same level as where it opened. Due to this, a Doji pattern will always look like a simple dash (-). When a Doji has wicks, it will look like a cross, although the horizontal line will vary in position. The fact that the price opened and closed at the same price means that the bulls are bears were equal in strength. In addition, a Doji is neither a bullish nor bearish candlestick. As such, it is seen as a sign of indecision. When it happens, the trader has to wait for other signs to know where the market will move. You will find that the market might reverse or continue strongly in the same direction after a Doji has formed.

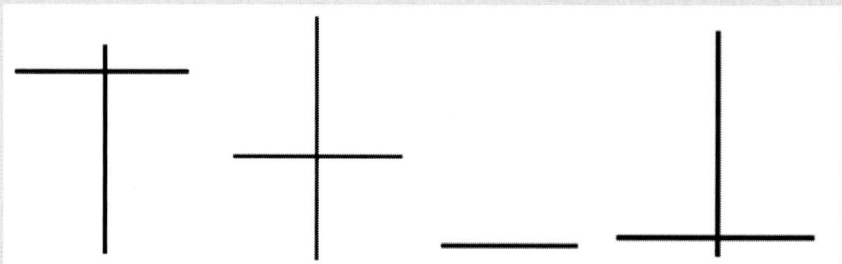

*Common Doji formations*

Go back to your MT5, and try to find some dojis in the charts. What happened after the Doji?

## Spinning Top

A spinning top is a candlestick with a very small body and wicks that are longer than the body on either side. Spinning tops indicate intense fighting between the bulls and bears, usually ending in a draw. In short, a spinning top shows that neither buyers nor sellers are in control of the market. Unlike the Doji, a spinning top can be bearish or bullish.

All the same, if a spinning top occurs when the price is moving up (uptrend), it might indicate that the buyers are becoming weaker, and the market might reverse and start moving down (downtrend). Similarly, if it occurs when the price is in a downtrend, it could mean that the sellers are getting exhausted, and that price might reverse into an uptrend.

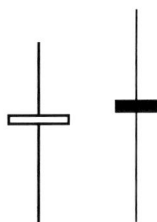

*Spining tops*

Open your charts and try to find some spinning tops. See what happened in the market after they were formed.

## Marubozu

Do not mind some of these new candlestick names that you might have never heard before, like *Doji* and *Marubo-zu*. They are Japanese names, having been coined by the inventor of candlesticks. So, in addition to day trading, you are also learning a little bit of Japanese.

Well, Marubozu is another type of candlestick that is very easy to spot. They appear as candles with bodies and no wicks at all. They can be bullish or bearish.

When a Marubozu appears, it shows that either the buying or selling activity was very strong. A bullish Marubozu shows that the price opened low and went high without being pushed down at all. As such, there were very few sellers, or they were overpowered. In the same way, a bearish Marubozu tells us that the sellers were very powerful that the buyers were not able to push the price any higher.

A Marubozu is considered to be a continuation pattern because, when it happens, the dominant trend at that time continues.

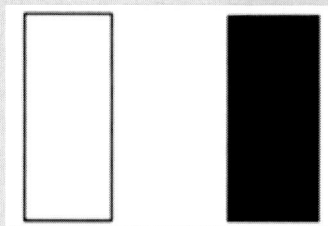

*Marubozu candlesticks*

## Hanging Man

A hanging man candlestick formation is a bearish candlestick that has a small body, little or no small wick at the top, and a very long wick on the bottom.

When it forms during an uptrend, it might predict a reversal of the trend. In short, the market might start falling. Try to verify this information by looking at where a hanging man was formed during a rising market.

*Hanging man candlestick pattern*

## HAMMER

A hammer candlestick looks like the hanging man, only that it is a bullish candle and is only relevant when it forms during a downtrend. It has a small body with a little or no wick at the top and a very long wick at the bottom.

If it forms during a downtrend, it might be an indication that the trend might reverse, and an uptrend will start.

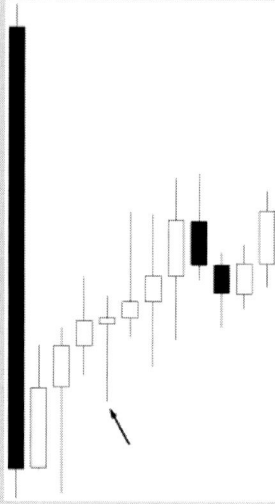

*Hammer candlestick pattern*

## SHOOTING STAR

The shooting star and inverted hammer look like the hanging man and hammer placed upside-down.

The shooting star is a bearish candlestick with a small body, a long wick at the top, and a tiny or no wick on the lower side. This formation is only relevant during a bullish trend, and, when it happens, it is an indication that the trend might reverse.

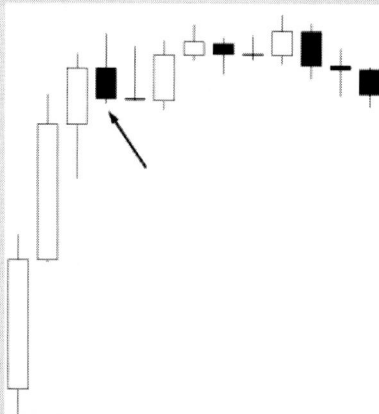

*Shooting star candlestick formation*

## INVERTED HAMMER

An inverted hammer is only relevant if it forms during a downtrend. It is a bullish candlestick that shows a potential reversal of a downtrend to an uptrend. It has a small body, a long upper wick, and a tiny or no wick on the lower side.

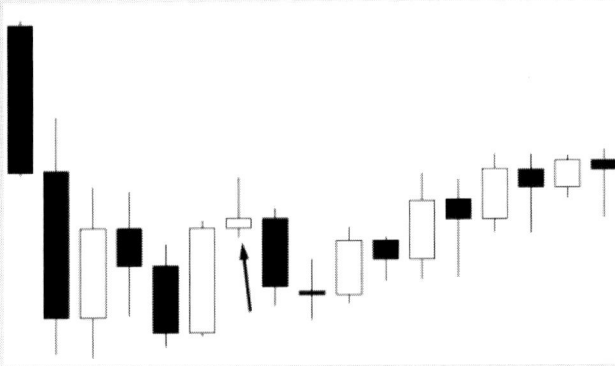

*Inverted hammer candlestick*

## *Double Candlestick Patterns*

Have you seen the magic that happens after the above single-candle patterns are formed? Yes, they work!

If you have been impressed by the magic of the single-candle patterns, then prepare to be blown away by the power of double-candle patterns. You will realize that the patterns with more candles are more powerful. Let us see if this fact is true.

## BULLISH ENGULFING PATTERN

A bullish engulfing pattern is made up of two candlesticks. The bearish candlestick must be on the left side and the bullish one on the right. The distinguishing feature of a bullish engulfing pattern is that the bullish candle should have a bigger body than the bearish one and completely engulf (cover it).

This pattern is only relevant during a downtrend market and will usually imply that the trend might reverse into an uptrend.

*Bullish engulfing pattern*

## BEARISH ENGULFING PATTERN

A bearish engulfing pattern is the opposite of a bullish engulfing pattern. It is formed when a bullish candle on the left is completely covered by a larger bearish candle on the right.

This pattern is only valid when it happens during an uptrend and usually predicts the end of the uptrend and the beginning of a downtrend.

*Bearish engulfing pattern*

## Tweezer Tops

A tweezer top pattern is formed when a bullish candle with a small body, small upper wick, and no lower wick appears, followed by a bearish candle with a small body, small upper wick, and no wick on the lower end. In short, the two candles must be similar, only differing in the sense that one is bullish, and the other is bearish.

The pattern is only valid when it occurs during an uptrend and usually signals that the trend is becoming weak and might reverse into a downtrend.

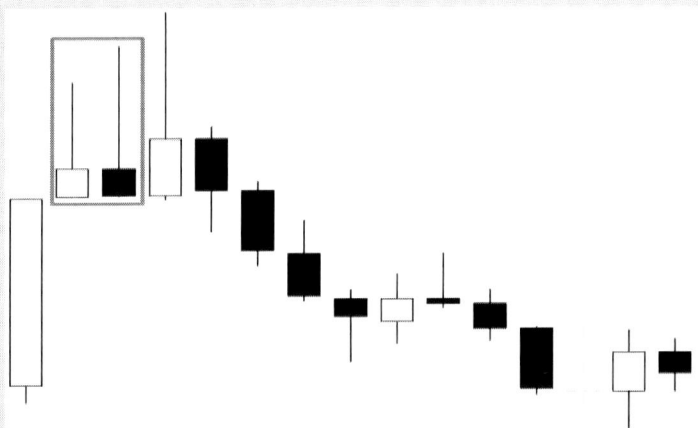

*Tweezer tops formation*

## Tweezer Bottoms

A tweezer bottom formation is the opposite of the tweezer top pattern. It consists of a bearish candle on the left with a small body, no wick at the top, and a long wick on the bottom, followed by a bullish candle with a small body, no wick at the top, and a long wick at the bottom.

A tweezer bottom is only relevant when it forms during a downtrend. It signals a possible end of the downtrend and the beginning of an uptrend.

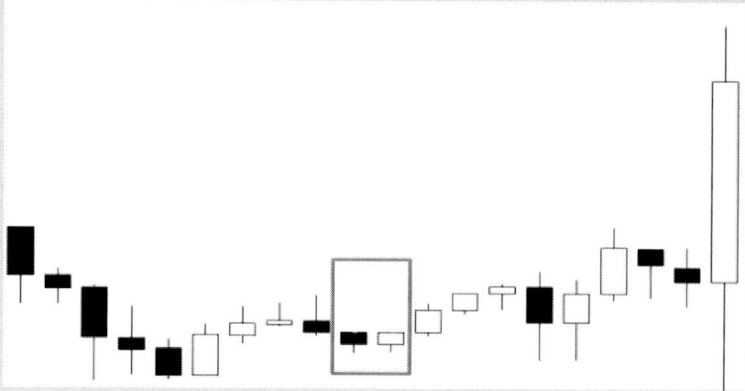

*Tweezer bottoms pattern*

### Triple Candlestick Patterns

As you keep trying to find these interesting candle-stick patterns in your charts, you might have noticed that double-candle formations are harder to find. That is true. However, it is more of a good thing because it means that when one of them shows up, something is going to happen in the near future. You should, there-fore, be very keen when watching your charts because the patterns are very rare to find and missing out on one means losing a good trading opportunity.

In this part, we are going to look at the most powerful three-candle patterns that we can use in day trading.

### Evening Star

The evening star pattern is formed by three candles. There should be a good-sized bullish candle (not a Do-ji) on the left, followed by a much smaller bullish candle in the middle, and on the right, a good-sized bearish candle that is bigger than half of the candle on the left.

This pattern is valid when it forms during an uptrend. It signifies a possible end to the trend and a reversal into a downtrend.

*Evening star pattern*

## MORNING STAR

A morning star formation is the opposite of the evening star pattern. It consists of a good-sized bearish candle on the left, a much smaller bearish candle in the middle, and a good-sized bullish candlestick on the right. The bullish candle must be more than half the size of the candle on the left.

The pattern is valid when it forms during a downtrend. It notifies a trader of a potential end of the downward movement and the possible start of an uptrend.

*Morning star pattern*

## THREE BULLISH SOLDIERS

The three bullish soldiers candlestick pattern consists of three bullish candles. The first candle should be small, followed by a bigger bullish candle that has a tiny wick at the top, and, finally, a much bigger bullish candle that has tiny or no wicks at all.

This is a reversal pattern that should only be used during a downtrend. When it appears, it signifies that the falling trend is becoming weak, and the bulls are becoming stronger.

*Three bullish soldiers*

## THREE BEARISH SOLDIERS

The three bearish soldiers pattern formation is the direct opposite of the three bullish soldiers pattern. It consists of three bearish candlesticks where the one on the left is small, followed by a bigger candle with small wicks then finally a bigger candle with little or no wicks.

This pattern is only relevant during an uptrend. When it is formed, it is an indication that the trend is becoming weak and that a downtrend might begin soon. The growing bear candles show that the sellers are becoming stronger.

*Three bearish soldiers*

## RISING THREE

The rising three candlestick formation is made up of five candles, although only three are the most important. It consists of three small bearish candles sandwiched between two huge bullish candlesticks. The candlestick on the right must close higher than the huge candle on the left.

This pattern is only valid during rising markets (uptrend), and when it occurs, it signifies a continuation of the existing trend.

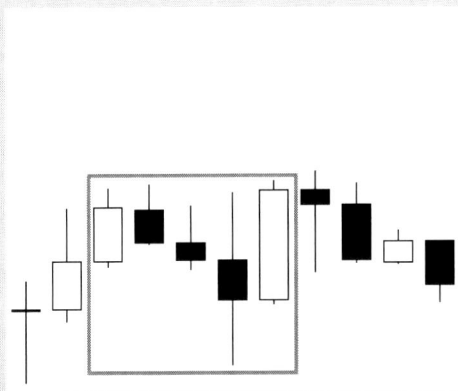

*Rising three pattern*

## FALLING THREE

Just like the rising three candlesticks pattern, the falling three formation is also made up of five candles. However, this time, there are three small bullish candles enclosed within two huge bearish candles. The bearish candle to the right of the pattern should close lower than the first huge bearish candle.

The falling three method is used during downtrends only. When it occurs, it means that the downtrend is likely to continue.

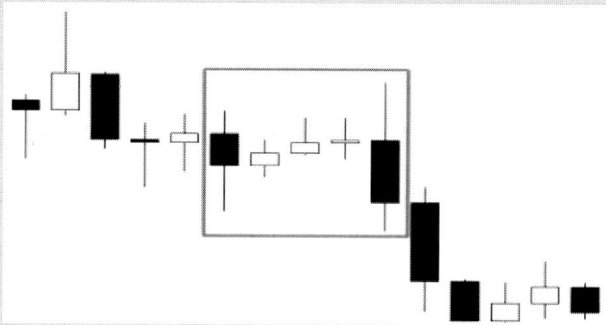

*Falling three pattern*

## SUMMARY

Voila! You have just completed your first charting lesson! How was it? Did you try to find these amazing patterns in your MT5 charts?

Well, candlesticks are the first step toward understanding and analyzing the markets; however, you can use the information that you have already learned to try and trade. I mean, you can now wait for the patterns to form and see how the prices move afterward. We cannot use past formations since the preceding market movements already left us. However, from now on, use the demo Metaquotes MT5 and capital to sell or buy when you see any of these patterns forming.

To place a trade, click on the button at the top-left side of the window where you will see the pattern(s) forming. Click the "Sell" button if you see that a down-trend has formed or the "Buy" button if an uptrend has formed. Keep in mind that you are just getting started, so if you make losses, it does not mean that you are already losing. You still have a long way to go, and the process will only get more interesting.

In conclusion, I hope you enjoyed this lesson and that you were able to find all of the patterns inside your charts. I understand that the three-candle patterns are harder to occur, and that is pretty normal. Feel free to use any tradable instrument on your platform. Like we said in the beginning, the lessons that you will be getting can be applied in any market.

# CHAPTER 9
## SUPPORT AND RESISTANCE

Any time people are trying to explain trading, they like to advise others to "buy low and sell high." This is a very true and important fact, but the biggest problem is that there is usually no clear explanation on how to find the highs and lows. In this section of the book, we are going to learn how to find the best areas for buying and selling.

Dear reader, welcome to another of trading's most important concepts: support and resistance.

## WHAT ARE SUPPORT AND RESISTANCE?

In general, support and resistance zones are the areas in the market where a commodity is expected to exhibit interesting behavior. In most cases, the expected behavior at these zones is opposition. In trading, this opposition is known as "rejection." In short, when the price touches the zones, it might be reversed in the opposite direction. So, if a certain index was rising, when it gets to an important zone of opposition, it might slow down and change into a downtrend. Similarly, a stock that has been moving down might get to a special zone then slow down and turn. At times, the markets choose to be defiant, and they oppose the rejection then move past these important zones.

The market is always a battlefield for buyers and sellers. Just like in any war, each side has its territory, and when the enemy goes closer to their opponent's territory, they risk losing the war. We also have this concept in the market, where the sellers and buyers have their territory. So, at times, the market will go into the sellers' territory, and since they are very strong there, they will send it down. On the other hand, when the market goes near the buyers' areas, they will ambush it by buying heavily. The result will be a rising market.

## Support

Support areas are the ones that are below the current position of the market, where the price is likely to slow down, reverse, or take time to break. It is known as a support zone because it attempts to keep the market from going any lower. In these zones, there are many buyers who are waiting for the market to get there, so they can buy it. If you can go back a few lessons back, remember we said that the market tends to repeat its history. Therefore, traders will look at their charts and identify the best support zones then wait for the price to get there. When it does, they will use more analytical tools like reversal or continuation candlestick patterns and then buy once they get the confirmation.

Below is an image showing support zones in a market.

*Support zones*

From the above image, you can see that when the price reached the support zones, it would bounce and go up. This is because many buyers watch these important areas, and they place buy trades there.

### Resistance

Resistance zones are the areas above the current market position where the price is likely to slow down, reverse, or take time to break. They are known as resistance zones since they attempt to prevent the market from going any higher. Resistance areas are the strongholds of sellers. As such, when the market reaches these zones, there are chances that many sellers will execute sell trades and send the market back down. Just like the support zones, traders will identify the areas of resistance then wait for the price to touch them. After this, they can apply more analytical tools, and, if appropriate for them, they will open sell trades.

Here is an image showing resistance zones in the gold market.

*Resistance zones*

As you can tell from the image, the price would go down after touching the important resistance zones. This is because many traders are always on the lookout at these levels, and, when the price gets to them, they execute sell trades.

Now that you know what the terms support and resistance mean, it is time to go to your charts and mark as many support and resistance zones as you can see.

## HOW TO IDENTIFY SUPPORT AND RESISTANCE ZONES

If you did the exercise of identifying these zones in your charts, you probably realized that some of them are very small, while others are big. For the sake of the accuracy and reliability of your trading signals, we are only going to look at the strongest zones.

So, how do we tell when a zone is strong?

### *Repetition*

The first method of identifying the strongest support and resistance zones is looking at how many times the market reached the area and got rejected. Minor zones are touched only once, and then you see that the price broke them later on. On the other hand, the stronger zones are touched by price numerous times, and they reject the price, or it takes multiple attempts before the price eventually moves past them. The more times that a zone is tested by price, the stronger it becomes.

Let us look at an example of a strong resistance zone.

*A strong resistance zone*

The above image shows a strong resistance area marked by the red rectangle. We refer to it as a strong resistance zone because the market attempted to break it numerous times but failed.

In area 1, we see that the market tried to break it strongly, but the sellers refused to let the price rise any higher. In areas 2, 3, and 5, the market went down immediately; it touched the resistance. In area 4, the sellers were too anxious to sell, and they did it even before the zone was touched.

*Note*: Support and resistance zones are not lines. Therefore, when drawing them, perceive them as zones (wide areas). Use the rectangle tool in your MT5 to draw the strong zones. To do so, click on "insert," then "objects," then "shapes" choose the "rectangle" option. Click and drag inside the chart to draw your zones.

Here is an example of a strong resistance zone.

*A strong support zone*

In the figure above, we can tell that the zone is quite strong, as it was tested five times. In areas 1 and 2, the price touched the zone and slowed down. It did not bounce back up or break the zone downward. In area 3, it touched the zone and went up before testing the support zone again at zone 4. Between zones 4 and 5, it slowed down before the bulls initiated a strong up-trend. In this case, we say that the bulls won the war.

## Candlestick formations

The second way to identify and validate strong support and resistance zones is by looking at how candlesticks behave when they touch the zones.

### REJECTIONS

The most interesting and revealing tell-tale sign that the market has hit a strong zone is that the candlesticks will have very long wicks. If you refer to the two images above, you will see that when the market touches a resistance zone, it mostly forms very long wicks on the upper side. Do you remember what wicks mean? Yes, the long wicks on the upper side mean that the bulls tried to push the price higher, but the bears would not allow them, so they pushed the prices lower.

The same holds for the support zone. You can see that when the price touched it, the candlesticks formed long wicks on the lower side. This means that the bears tried to push the prices lower, but the bulls would not let them. Since this is a bullish stronghold, the bears lost the battle, and the prices went up.

### Shorter Candles

Another indication that the prices have hit a major zone is that the candlesticks start becoming shorter (smaller). They have small bodies and wicks. The explanation is quite simple: traders are always looking at the important levels in the market. Therefore, when the price goes near, say, a resistance zone, those who had bought trades close them since they expect prices to reverse. This causes the volume in the market to decrease, thus the minimal trading activity shown by the short candles.

The short candles also show that the bulls and bears are waiting for each other to make a move so they can oppose it. At this time, nobody wants to buy or sell. However, once a definite direction has been established, the candles start growing.

Go back to the above charts and see if this is true. Also, check the areas where you drew the support and resistance zones in your MT4 charts. Does this concept apply? Of course, it does.

To this end, you are now able to identify the strongest support and resistance zones in the market. Next, let us see why these zones are very important in day trading.

## USES OF SUPPORT AND RESISTANCE ZONES

### *Selling High, Buying Low*

Finally, you get to understand this overused phrase in the trading industry. It is very simple: when you see the price approaching a support zone, you should always expect a potential bullish move. We say 'potential' because nothing in the market is assured. The price might get to the support zone and choose to slow down, bounce, or break it and continue going lower. What I am trying to say is that you should never be caught buying at a resistance level or selling at an area of support.

It is always advisable to move with the majority of the traders. In fact, big players such as market makers use these points to take our money. Ignorant traders who fail to adhere to this rule usually end up with losses. Concisely, practice hard to identify the strongest zones and wait for the markets to touch them before making any trading decision.

### *Identifying Market Direction*

Market direction, popularly known as "trend" in trading, is one of the most important concepts that you must follow for you to succeed in this industry. Just like you should sell at resistance zones and buy at support areas, you should always trade along the main market direction. You cannot be trying to sell when the majority of traders and the big players are pushing the market up. There is a common phrase that you will hear traders throwing around; that the trend is your best friend.

Many traders hear about this concept, but they fail since they do not understand how to identify the main trend. Luckily for you, this guide will show you the best way to do it.

Now, in the market, there are things known as peaks and troughs. The peaks are the highest points that you can see the market reaching before turning back. Troughs are the lowest points that the market reaches before going back up. Both of these are minor support and resistance points. If you connect the points using straight lines, you will end up with a zigzag formation.

DOWNTREND

UPTREND

*Peaks and troughs*

- ### *Uptrend*

When the peaks are formed in higher succession, we say the market is in an uptrend. If a new peak is formed higher than the previous one, we call it a higher-high. During an uptrend, the troughs are also formed in higher succession. In short, each new trough is positioned higher than the previous one. When this happens, we say a higher-low has been formed. Collectively, when a market is forming higher Highs and higher Lows concurrently, then an uptrend is formed. During this time, you should only look for buy trades.

- **Downtrend**

A downtrend happens when the market starts making lower peaks and lower troughs in succession. In short, when a trough is formed lower than the previous one, we have a descending zigzag direction that we call a downtrend. During a downtrend market direction, lower Highs and lower Lows are formed. In a downtrend, you should only be looking for sell trades.

- **Ranging Market**

There are times when the market is neither moving up nor down. When this happens, it is because it has become trapped between two support and resistance zones. We refer to this as a "ranging" or "sideways" market since price movement is fixed between two points that form a range between them. You might think that since the market is ranging, trading has to stop. Wrong! Once you identify and validate a ranging market, you can take advantage of the movements between the two zones to make some money. However, many seasoned traders advise beginners not to trade ranging markets to avoid being trapped on the wrong side once a breakout occurs.

*A ranging market*

### Confluence

In trading, confluence happens when two or more analytical tools predict the same thing. For example, the evening star candlestick pattern (possible downtrend) may form at a resistance level. In this case, we have two tools that are telling us that the trend of the market that we are looking at might start going down.

Now, support and resistance should be mandatory tools in your trading. Once you have set up the candlestick chart, start identifying the most important support and resistance zones in the market. From there, use the zones to build up confluence. You can look or wait for candlestick patterns to form on the identified levels. A trading signal that is supported by both of these tools increases the likelihood of being profitable.

As you read further, you will get to know more tools that can be used to build up confluence. The more confirmations that you get about a potential trading signal, the more confidence you will gain, not to mention that it might turn out to be a great trading opportunity.

### Entry, Exit, Stop Levels

Support and resistance zones are very important when it comes to managing your trades. You cannot go into the market blindly without knowing where you should hunt for trades and where to exit. A real trader needs to know where the market is heading before they execute any trade. In addition, they should be able to tell when the signal that they have taken is wrong so they can exit the trade(s) without incurring further losses.

• **Entry**

Support and resistance help us to know where to expect trading opportunities. We have already discussed this. The first golden rule in entering a trade is to know whether the market is going up, down, or ranging. The second rule is identifying support and resistance zones to know whether you should buy or sell. In an uptrend, only wait to buy when you have a support zone. Similarly, during a downtrend, only wait to sell at a support zone.

- *Exit*

Before executing a trade, you must know where you expect the market to go. In so doing, you will know where to take your profits and run. Support and resistance will help you to do this. If you have spotted a buy trade, you should expect to get out when the market approached the next level of resistance. You do not want to stay in a trade for too long such that the market gives you profits, then it hits an area of resistance and falls back to take them all back.

Therefore, mark the possible reversal points of the market using support and resistance zones. You can place your take-profits at these levels or manually wait for the prices to get there, then you can exit the trades manually.

- *Stop Levels*

At times, you will analyze the market and spot a potential trade signal. Unfortunately, once you are already in the trade, the market will not go as per your anticipation, and you will start making some losses. This is normal in trading, and you should accept it. What matters is that you should make more profits than losses. We shall cover this topic wider under Risk Management later in the guide.

So, when a trade has turned against us, and we start making losses, what do we do? Should we let it run and hope that it will favor us later, or do we exit the trade immediately?

The answer is none of the above.

For one, we can never be too sure about the direction of the markets, as they are influenced by hundreds of factors that we cannot control. As such, before executing a trade, we must know where to place our stop-loss. If you recall what a stop-loss is, it is a type of order that automatically closes a losing trade when a trade goes against a trade.

Traders use previous support and resistance levels to place their stop-loss. So, let us assume that you have spotted a potential sell trade that has formed a confluence between a resistance zone and a bearish engulfing candlestick pattern. You will place your stop-loss a little distance above the resistance zone that you are using to trade.

Here is an image for a better explanation:

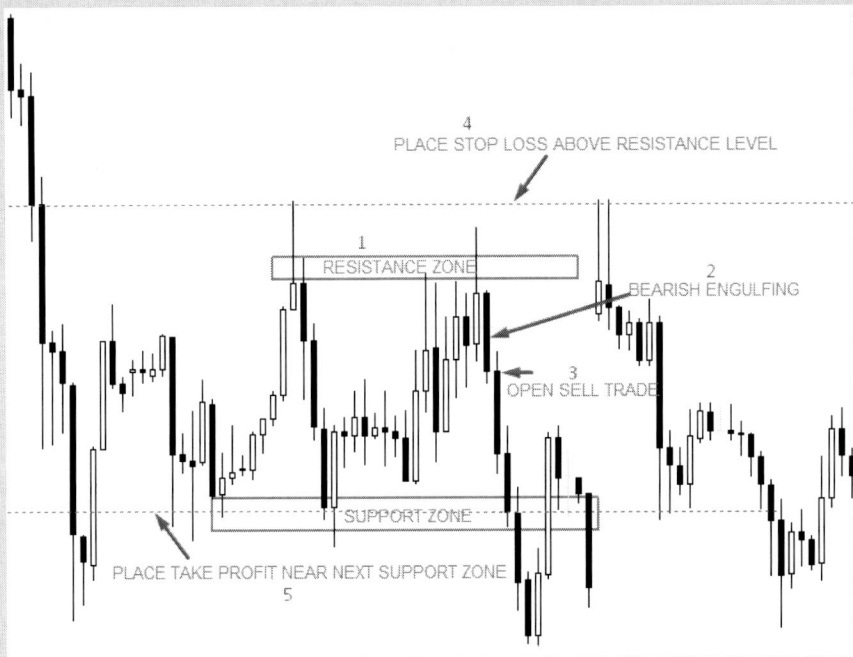

*Entry, exit, and stop-loss using support and resistance*

In the figure above, we can see from the extreme left that the market was moving in a downtrend since it was forming lower Highs and lower Lows. At point 1, we drew a resistance when the price reached the zone, and a rejection candle was formed. The market went down and later came to touch the zone again. Let us assume that we had been watching the market all that time.

At point 2, the market formed a bearish engulfing pattern after touching the resistance level. As such, we had a good confluence point here. So we decided to take the trade after the engulfing pattern was formed, and the candle had closed (point 3).

As we opened the trade, we were sure that it was during a downtrend, so the price was likely to go down. As such, we placed our stop-loss (5) near the next important support zone since we expected the price to pause or reverse there.

Similarly, we placed a protective stop-loss above the sell order and the resistance zone that gave us the trade (point 4). This is to close the trade in case the market broke past the zone and formed an uptrend. Please note that the stop-loss is placed beyond the resistance zone to prevent it from being executed in case the buyers attempt to push prices higher and get rejected.

**Note:** The stop-loss should neither be placed too close to the zone nor too far from it. If placed too close, it might be activated too early and lead to unnecessary losses. It should be allowed a little distance to allow the market some breathing space. Similarly, placing it too far from the zone can lead to excess losses.

If we had taken that trade, you could see that it went down immediately after the bearish engulfing pattern and into the support zone down below. It would have reached our take-profit order, and that would have made it a winning (profitable) trade since it hit the target and not the stop-loss. We won!

## SUMMARY

I hope you enjoyed yet another interesting lesson on chart analysis and finding the best trading opportunities. You now have two lethal weapons in your trading arsenal: candlestick formations, as well as support and resistance. I cannot stress enough how important these two concepts are in any form of trading. You already have enough tools to start day trading! All the same, in the next chapter, we shall look at more tools that can help with better chart analysis and identifying profitable trading opportunities.

In the meantime, put the skills that you have acquired so far to use. Draw those zones and wait for candlestick patterns to confirm the trades for you. When you spot a qualified signal, do not hesitate to take it. More importantly, make sure you know where to place your take-profit and stop-loss orders.

# CHAPTER 10
## CHART INDICATORS

In the past two chapters, we have looked at two major concepts that can be used in analyzing the market and using price action to enter trades, as well as manage. Before we look at more day trading strategies, we need to study a special group of chart analysis tools known as indicators.

Indicators are automated tools that are applied in the charts to reveal information that can be hard to spot with the naked eye. The indicators appear in different shapes and sizes on top of the charts in the trading platforms. We need indicators because charts show much more information than just support and resistance zones or reversal and continuation of trends. As such, by using automated tools, our analysis can improve.

While indicators are meant to enhance one's trading accuracy and confluence, they should never be used as the sole analytical tools. One of the worst mistakes that newbie traders make is applying as many indicators in their charts as they can and using them to make their trading decisions. Do not make this mistake. You should base all your trading on pure price action, which is studying market formations using support and resistance, trends, and candlestick patterns. When it comes to indicators, only use them to build more confluence or reveal hidden information that you can interpret to make better trading decisions.

## TYPES OF INDICATORS

If you ever went out there to look for indicators, you would never have enough time and space to store them because there are millions of them. Your trading platform will come with some pre-installed ones. These are very basic ones, but they show the most important information so you might not need to go looking for more. In fact, the basic indicators are the ones used as reference points in the making of the other indicators that you will find being sold or freely available online.

No matter how many indicators we have in existence, all of them can be classified into four categories, namely trend, volume, momentum, and volatility indicators. The indicators in the four groups can be further classified into two groups of either lagging or leading indicators

A lagging indicator is one that shows information that has already passed. For instance, a lagging indicator can show that a reversal has already happened. On the other hand, a leading indicator tries to predict the future price behavior of the market. For example, a leading indicator can tell us that a trend is about to end.

The four main types of indicators are:

- **Trend**

Trend indicators try to reveal the direction of the market (trend) or if there is no movement at all. If used properly, trend indicators can help a trader to know which direction to trade in or whether to stay out of the market.

Some examples of trend indicators are the moving average, Ichimoku Kinko Hyo, parabolic SAR, and MACD.

Trend indicators are lagging indicators.

- **Volume**

Volume indicators tally the information in the market and reveal the power of the bulls versus bears in the market. In short, they tell us the units of the trading instrument being sold or bought at a given time. You can find better trades by trading when the volume of bulls or bears is increasing (depending on whether you are buying or selling).

Some examples of volume indicators are Chaikin Money Flow, On-Balance-Volume, and Klinger Volume Oscillator.

Volume indicators can be lagging or leading, depending on the one being used.

- **Momentum**

Momentum indicators show the strength of a trend and whether a reversal is likely to occur. They are very useful in finding peaks and troughs. As such, they can be useful in knowing when or where to enter or exit a trade.

Some examples of momentum indicators are the Average Directional Index (ADX), Relative Strength Index (RSI), and the Stochastic.

These indicators are leading.

- **Volatility**

Volatility indicators show us the rate of price changes in the market at a specific time. Volatility is important since we need the markets to move so we can ride trends and make some profits. A higher volatility means the prices are moving fast, so the market is trending well.

Some examples of volatility indicators include Bollinger Bands and Average True Range.

Volatility indicators are lagging indicators.

## POPULAR CHART INDICATORS

Below, we shall look at one example of an indicator from each of the four categories and how they can be used in day trading.

First, you need to have the chart of the trading instrument that you need to analyze open then follow the following steps:

- In your MT5, click on the "View" menu at the top of the program

- Next, click on "Navigator." A panel will open to the left side. It contains folders that have the indicators inside.

- From here, you need to choose the type of indicator that you want to apply. If it is a trend indicator, click on the (+) sign next to the "Trend Folder" in the panel. It will open a list of trend indicators.

- To add any of the trend indicators to your active chart, click and drag it into the chart, then press "okay." The indicator will appear in your chart.

- To remove an indicator from the chart, right-click inside the open window, click on the "indicator list," then click on the indicator that you want to remove and press "delete."

You will do the same when attaching or removing the other indicators. Just look inside the relevant folders, then drag the indicators into the chart you want to analyze.

### The Moving Average (Trend)

Attach the moving average to your chart. It will appear as a line.

The moving average, popularly known as the MA, is the most common indicator used in trading. It is very useful in that it reveals price action by filtering out the noise from the market through smoothing. As you can see from your chart, the MA sometimes goes up, down, or stays in a straight line.

MAs use a parameter known as "periods" in displaying the price action. The period refers to the number of days that the indicator will look into the past and then smooth the closing prices to give you a line that shows us the market direction. You can edit the period to be used by going to indicator list > moving average, then under "Parameters," edit the number of days that you need under "Period." When you click "OK," the moving average will be displayed.

When the period is too low, the MA will be very sensitive to price and will show a line that follows almost every move of the market. If the period is increased, the displayed MA smoothens and shows the average direction of the market. The most common periods used in MAs are 21, 50, 120, and 200.

Let us attach a 21 and 50-period MA to our charts and see how they look.

*21 and 50-period moving averages*

## INTERPRETING MAS

From the image above, you can see that the 21-period MA reacts more to price than the 50-period MA. To read the trend, we look at the position of the market in relation to the MA's position. If the price is above the MA, then we have an uptrend. When the price is below the MA, then we have a downtrend. You can use any period of your choice alongside the previous tools that we learned.

Have you realized what happens when the two MAs cross? Look again! On the left side of the above image, you can see that when the 21 MA crossed above the 50 MA, the price went up. Similarly, when the 21 crossed below the 50 on the right side, we had a smooth down-trend movement. So, you use single MAs or MA cross-overs to confirm candlestick patterns or support and resistance signals.

## Bollinger Bands (Volatility)

Remove the MAs from your chart and attach the Bollinger Bands (BB). You will find it under the "Examples" folder in the Navigator window.

The BB is yet another favorite indicator used by traders. It consists of a moving average placed between two lines on either side. The two outer lines are known as the bands. Bollinger Bands are used in revealing the volatility in the market as well as the trend and future areas of support and resistance. As you can tell, it is an all-around system. However, you should never use it as the sole guide in your trading; remember that price action remains the best lead.

Here is a BB attached to a chart:

*The Bollinger Bands indicator*

## INTERPRETING BOLLINGER BANDS

The two outer bands show the volatility in the market. When they come close together, it means there is minimal volatility (price movement). You can see that even the candles formed in such areas are small. On the other hand, when the bands expand and move away from each other, it means there is a lot of volatility in the market.

This indicator has many interesting uses. It can also be used in trading-ranging markets. If you have already spotted a ranging market using our previous tools, attach the bands to your chart. You can look at what we call the "Bollinger Bounce" to trade a stagnant market. During these periods, the price will tend to touch any of the outer bands and then return to the MA in the middle. As such, you can confirm your trades using this indicator.

The other way you can trade using BBs is to wait for breakouts when the market is trending. If the price breaks out of the upper bands, there are chances that an uptrend will continue. Similarly, if the price breaks out of the lower band, then expect a downtrend. A "break" means that the body of a candlestick is closed outside any of the bands. Do not consider the wicks. I will never get tired of reminding you to only use indicators as confirmations of potential trade opportunities that you have spotted using candlestick formations and support and resistance zones.

*Note*: You can tweak the parameters of the BB to suit your trading style. Go to "Indicator List" > "BB"> "Inputs" and play around with the numbers.

### *Relative Strength Index (Momentum)*

Our third chart indicator is known as the Relative Strength Index, RSI. It appears on a different window below the chart of the instrument being traded. The RSI is simply a line that oscillates between two levels (0 and 100). There are two more levels between the 0 and 100 marked as 70 and 30. These are the ones that we shall pay more attention to.

Let us see how the RSI looks in the charts.

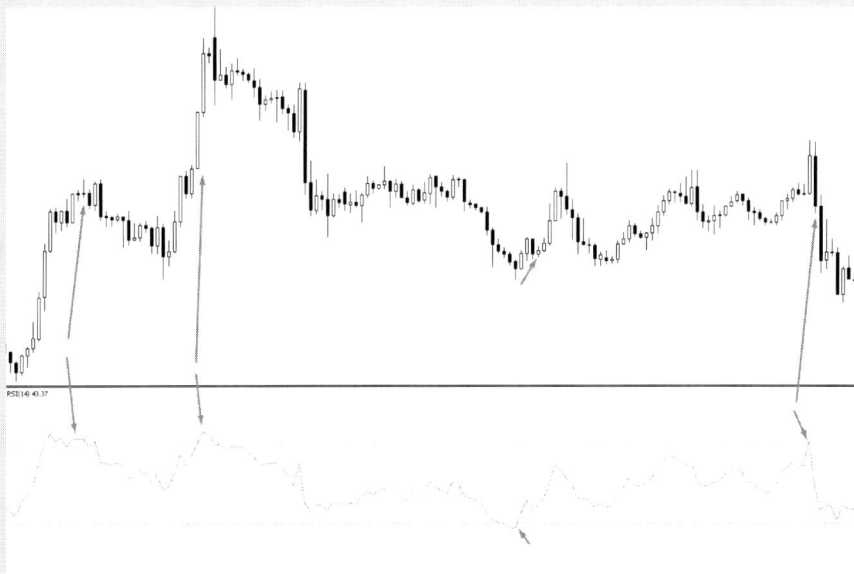

*The RSI indicator*

## INTERPRETING THE RSI

The RSI tries to show us when the market is overbought or oversold so we can expect reversals. When the blue line touches the upper (70) mark, the market is said to be overbought. In short, the bulls have utilized all their buying power so they might not push the market any higher. When the line touches the lower mark (30), the market is said to be oversold and might reverse soon. Here, the bears have utilized much of their selling power, so the market might not sink any further.

Due to this predictive power, the RSI is used in finding tops and bottoms. You can see from the above image that when the price touched the overbought line, it would fall later. Similarly, when it touched the oversold line, the price would rise in the future.

### On-Balance Volume (Volume)

Our final chart indicator is known as the On-Balance Volume, OBV. As the name suggests, it is a volume indicator and will reveal whether the bulls or bears are in charge of a market. Reading the OBV is very simple since all you need to do is to look at the sharp tops and bottoms that it forms. Next, you should draw a line to connect only the very dominant tops and bottoms. Look at the image below.

*The OBV indicator*

### Interpreting the OBV

When observing the tops and bottoms, identify where they are forming higher Highs and lower Lows or lower Highs and lower Lows. Next, use the "Draw Trendline" tool found at the top-left side of your MT5 to join these important points.

If the resulting trendline is sloping up, then there is a more bullish volume. In this case, you should only look for buy trades. If the trendline is sloping downward, then there is more bearish volume, so you should only look for sell trades.

## SUMMARY

Your trading arsenal is growing!

Indicators are very useful tools when they are used appropriately. Unfortunately, some trainers and marketers mislead potential traders that there are magical indicators that can be used as standalone tools to spot accurate trades. I almost fell into that trap when I was starting out back in the day. Believe it or not, I spent over two years searching for the best indicator to make me a profitable trader, but I never came across even one!

In the end, I had to embrace the fact that I had always been told that price action is the best indicator of trading.

The four indicators that we have discussed here are drawn from each of the four categories. Therefore, if you included all of them in your chart, each of them would give you different information. If you add the information that they show you to the support and resistance zones, as well as candlesticks strategies, the trades that you spot will most likely be profitable.

Finally, you need to understand that there are more volume, momentum, trend, and volatility indicators that you can use. The four indicators that we used in this chapter are meant to show you how different indicators can show different market information. I also chose the four specifically because they are simple yet very efficient if you use them properly. In short, you can research more indicators and practice using them in your charts. The only warning that I would give is that indicators should never replace your price action skills!

In the following chapters, we shall discuss some of the best day trading strategies that you can use to make a living. They will combine price action, a few indicators, and, of course, new interesting trading skills.

# CHAPTER 11
## ELLIOT WAVES

In the early 1920s, when stock trading was still an emerging profession, a seasoned stock trader named Ralph Elliot made a wonderful discovery that changed the entire trading industry. After analyzing the market for over 70 years, he discovered that the markets do not move randomly but follow some repetitive cycles. He named these cycles "waves." According to Elliot, the upward and downward movements of the markets were based on the collective psychology of the traders, and by understanding this, predicting the markets would be easy.

## FRACTALS

To explain the wave theory, Elliot used fractals to explain the market. Fractals are objects or elements that can be split into parts, and the smaller resulting parts will be similar to the original object. For instance, if you split a snowflake, it will produce smaller snowflakes that will be similar to the larger one. Similarly, when a huge cloud breaks up, the smaller clouds that are born bear the same shape and color as the parent cloud.

According to Elliot, the markets also follow the same principle. Whenever there is an uptrend, there will be smaller uptrends inside the main trend. The same is true during a downtrend. Therefore, by identifying fractals, we can predict the direction of the market and trade according to the main trend.

## THE 5-3 WAVE PATTERN

This concept identified by Elliot came to be known as the "Elliot Wave Theory." It shows that when a market is trending, it follows something called the 5-3 wave pattern. In the pattern, there are two waves.

The first part of the pattern is made up of 5 waves that are known as the Impulse Waves. They move along the main trend.

The second part of the pattern is made up of 3 waves that are known as Corrective Waves. These waves move against the main trend.

Below is an image for a better understanding of this concept:

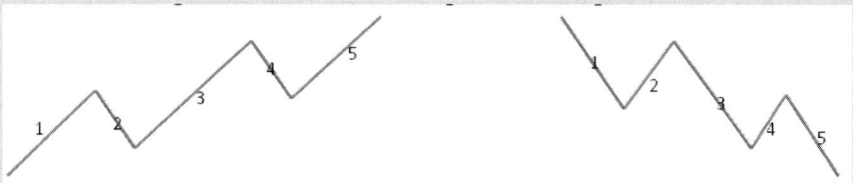

*Elliot waves showing an uptrend and downtrend*

In the image above, the wave on the left shows an uptrend. As you can see, there are 3 smaller waves that make up the larger upward movement. Waves 1, 3, and 5 move upward (impulse), while 2 and 4 oppose the main trend (corrective). Generally, the 5 waves work together to create an uptrend.

The image on the right shows a downtrend. Just like the one on the left, there are 3 impulse waves that follow the main downtrend and 2 corrective waves that oppose the main trend. Collectively, they create a downtrend.

Before we head over to the charts to try and identify the Elliot waves, here are the five cardinal rules used in identifying and validating the 5 waves:

- **Wave 1:** The first impulse wave is the beginning of a new trend. It happens when the traders in the market feel that the instrument is ready for buying or selling.

- **Wave 2:** After a small upward or downward movement, the traders who had started wave 1 might think the instrument is overvalued, so many will take profits. When this happens, the market will go up or down a little and form a short corrective wave. However, the new high or low that is formed can never be equal to the starting point of wave 1.

- **Wave 3:** When the new high or low is formed in wave 2 and fails to go past the starting point of wave 1, attentive traders realize that the instrument has established a new trend so they will place trades in huge numbers. This results in the formation of a very long wave 3. For this wave to be valid, it must move past the high or low formed by the end of wave 1. Wave 3 is usually the strongest and longest impulsive wave.

- **Wave 4:** After wave 3 has been active for some time, it becomes oversold or overbought (you can use an indicator to spot this). The reaction of most traders is to take the profits that wave 3 gave them before the market starts reversing. When they close their trades, the market reverses for a very short distance. However, trend traders know that the trend will continue, so they do not close their trades. This leads to the formation of a very short corrective wave 4 before the trend continues. Wave 4 is usually shorter than wave 2, but it should be higher than wave 2's ending point.

- **Wave 5:** Immediately wave 4 is completed; the final move of the trend starts forming. This is the wave where most of the traders who know how to study the market will place their trades. Wave 5 is usually driven by uncontrollable excitement known as hysteria. At times, impulse wave 5 will be very strong that it might be longer than wave 3. Since it is the last move in the trend, it tends to happen very fast. This is the time when most traders make or lose money.

- **The ABC wave:** At the end of wave 5, you might wonder what happens to the market. What happens is that if wave 5 was correctly identified, the overall trend starts reversing. In short, the 5-wave trend is corrected by a 3-wave countertrend formation.

The ABC wave that comes after wave 5 is also used in hunting for moves. In our case, though, we are going to stop at wave 5 since the moves that occur from the first wave to the last one are enough for day trading. In addition, the ABC wave can be a little confusing. For now, let us head over to the charts and try to identify some Elliot waves.

Below is an excellent Elliot wave in an uptrend.

*Below is an excellent Elliot wave during a downtrend.*

At this level, you have become an intermediate trader. Therefore, the above charts with Elliot waves should be self-explanatory. In your opinion, do the two waves in both charts adhere to the 5 rules of the Elliot wave theory? Second, are you able to spot the areas where you would have plotted your support and resistance zones? Are there any candlestick patterns in the turning points of the waves?

## TRADING WITH ELLIOT WAVES

Day trading is interesting, as you can tell from the lessons that you have received so far, right? This guide has simplified the best concepts of trading so that you understand and apply them without struggling. The best thing about the training that you are getting is that it uses price action and very basic tools to turn you into a professional day trader.

Now that you understand how the Elliot wave theory works, it is time to see how it can be used in trading using the concepts that you have acquired so far.

In the following sections, we shall use the two above charts with Elliot waves to see if all the concepts created confluence and gave us winning trades.

### Elliot Waves, Candlesticks, and Support & Resistance

A quick reminder here: when you open a new chart, the first thing that you should do is to identify and mark out the main areas of support and resistance. This is the first step in revealing the trend direction as well as where to look for potential trading signals. Refer back to the support and resistance chapter until you are able to identify these critical zones easily.

Now, our bullish chart with candlestick patterns and support and resistance included:

### DISCUSSION

Point 1 is our starting area. You can see from the left that we had a downtrend that was approaching the strong area of support below the market. Let us assume that we had been watching the price as it came to touch our support.

Upon hitting the support, you can see that the candles began decreasing in size, and long wicks were formed. These are signs of the price being rejected (bulls pushing the bears away, so they cannot take the market any lower). This is the first event that would have caught our attention. We can see that price tried to go higher, formed a Higher-High, then fell back to support where it faced more rejection and formed a Higher-Low. At this point, we had confirmed that wave 1 and wave 2 formations were in progress.

As the price bounced off the support for the second time, we would have been waiting for wave 2 to close, so we could enter the trade in the direction of the new trend (upward). A few candles later, we had a perfect three bullish soldiers pattern formed, and that confirmed that wave 2 was complete. After the last candle of the pattern closed, we would have entered the trade at the opening of the next candle, which was the start of wave 3.

Our stop-loss would go below the support level that gave us the entry while the take-profit would go in or near the next resistance zone. We would expect wave 3 to form near the next resistance area, which it did! We call this area, Take-Profit Level 1. This is because, as per the Elliot wave theory, a trend is not complete until it forms wave 5. As such, we would wait for wave 4 to pull back a little (correct). To identify the potential distance that the wave would correct, we look at the starting point of wave 2. Wave 3 should not reach that point. Second, we look to the left of the chart and identify a small support zone. That is where wave 4 is likely to end, and wave 5 would start.

In the image above, you can see that wave 4 obeyed

all these rules. It neither broke past the high of wave 1 nor the small area of support below it. In addition, it formed a bullish engulfing pattern, and wave 5 was confirmed. We could also have opened another buy here and placed our take-profit above the high of wave 3 and close to the next resistance zone. This would be our Take-Profit Level 3. Our stop-loss would be placed below the small support zone where wave 4 ended, and wave 5 began.

Assuming that we had taken both of these trades, we would have won in both. Do you see how the price took off and never went near our stop-loss levels?

Dear trader, this is how you read the market like an open book.

Next, we are going to dissect the bearish Elliot wave movement using candlestick patterns as well as support and resistance.

## DISCUSSION

Did you try to interpret this chart on your own?

As usual, we need to identify an existing trend that is headed toward a zone of support or resistance. In the above chart, we had an uptrend that had formed after bouncing off a support level. Let us assume that we had been watching the price rise. At the top of the chart, we had a strong resistance zone judging from the left side.

So, when the price touched the resistance zone, we see that it formed a bearish engulfing pattern. It went back up and formed some short candles, with the longer wicks appearing on the upper sides before another engulfing pattern was formed. Can you spot it? At this point, we do not have any wave 1 in sight. Price sank a little, and we would have thought that it had left without us. However, it reached a small support zone and bounced back into the resistance zone. We can see this from the rejection of the candles and the formation of a bullish engulfing pattern.

At this point, we have a clear impulse wave 1. The current wave would be corrective wave 2. We would watch to see if it would go higher than the start of wave 1, which it failed to do! Instead, the price faced massive rejection and later formed a huge bearish engulfing pattern. This is where we would mark the end of wave 2 and the beginning of the juicy wave 3. Our sell trade would be opened at the close of the last candle forming the bearish engulfing pattern.

As always, our protective stop-loss goes above the resistance level that gave us the trade. We are going to place our Take-Profit Level 1 in or near the next strong support area. As you can see, the price fell without going back to the stop-loss, and it would have hit our take-profit level very easily. At this level, we would have expected wave 3 to end and wave 4 to start the corrective movement.

Do you see how the market went into the support zone and looked like it had broken it without bouncing up? This is normal, and it only shows that the bears were very powerful. Again, we had a longer wave 3. Can you spot the small candles that started forming below the support area? Do you see that bullish engulfing pattern? The market rose again and went past our support. This was a clear wave 4 in progress. It went up until it met a small resistance zone, formed a huge wick that was followed by a clear bearish engulfing pattern.

This would mark the end of wave 4 and the start of wave 5. We would enter a second trade here (if we wanted) and placed our stop-loss slightly above the small resistance level where wave 4 ended. Our Take-Profit Level 2 would go below the point where wave 3 ended; that is in or near the next support level.

Just like our first trade, the second one would have also given us some easy, handsome profits that were almost risk-free.

### *Elliot Waves and Indicators*

The power of Elliot waves is endless. I believe that you can now identify them easily using their anatomy with the aid of trends, as well as support and resistance. We are now going to see how indicators can add to the accuracy of the Elliot waves using the same charts that we used above.

I will place three of the indicators that we looked at in the previous chapter in the same chart, so we can see what each one of them will be telling us. You can add the Bollinger Bands, RSI, and OBV indicators to your charts. I have not said the Moving Average because the BB already has a moving average in it.

A chart with the three indicators, support, and resistance zones, as well as our Elliot Wave, should look like this:

## Discussion

Sorry about the confusing chart above. The biggest reason that we discourage the use of too many indicators is that they can be confusing and misleading, and they also make the charts messy. However, pardon me for today because I had to bundle all of them into the charts, so we can discuss them all at once. Remember that you will have to choose the ones that you find most useful for your trading.

## Bollinger Bands

The BB has a Moving Average in the middle. I have set mine to period 21 so that it can react faster to the price and confirm my entries. We are day traders, so MAs with very low sensitivity might lead to missing trade opportunities. Look at where wave 1 ended and wave 2 began. Did the price break above the MA? No! Therefore, we had no permission to buy. The price was rejected, and it fell back to the support, and wave 2 ended as wave 3 began. This time, the price broke past the MA since a candle closed above it. As such, we would have taken our buy entry here.

At the same time, when the price was struggling to break the 21 MA, the bands of the BB were close together. However, when the MA was broken, the bands expanded. This is yet another confirmation since volatility had increased.

Finally, on the BB, do you see where the market touches the outer bands in the presence of our support and resistance zones? It is clear that those areas are very strong, and the market behaves as we would expect. You can see that it is at those points that the Elliot waves change from the impulse to corrective waves and vice-versa.

### RSI

The RSI is quite straightforward. Look at where wave 1 began. A few candles before, the RSI had touched the oversold (30) level. It told us to expect a new trend. Magically, the trend happened after some candles! However, we did not follow the RSI blindly; we waited for confirmation from candle patterns and the bounce from the support area.

Look at where wave 3 ended. The RSI was clearly in the overbought (70) level while coinciding with a resistance zone. As such, we had been expecting the market to slow down and reverse to form wave 4. Just like magic, the market pulled back, and we had our wave 4 formed! The next time that the RSI touched the overbought level, wave 5 had formed, and we would have taken our profits there.

## OBV

The OBV is also very simple yet very powerful. You can see that it began forming Higher-Highs and Higher-Lows when the price was at our support level and when the previous downtrend had ended. Therefore, in this area, we had the confluence from all our indicators that a new trend had started. With this information in mind, you would not find yourself trying to sell, as that would be opposing the trend. Also, the fact that the OBV told us about a new trend means that we caught the Elliot wave in its early stages of formation. As you can see from the indicator, the entire move was an uptrend as no Lower-Lows or Lower-Highs were formed.

## SUMMARY

Pat yourself on the back if this is how you would have had interpreted the above chart. You are now one of the best traders of your time just from the few lessons that you have received. I hope that you now believe that trading is not easy, but it can be made simple. To the untrained eye, all the concepts that you have studied would appear like Greek alphabets. However, to you, the newest trader on the block, you understand each and every one of them, courtesy of this guide. Now, all you need to do is to take your time and apply these concepts in live trading using your demo account. Consistent practice is the surest way to grasp and internalize your training. Persevere for now because soon, you will be able to spot these winning opportunities with utmost ease and precision.

Let us conclude this chapter by shouting together that, "*Elliot Waves are real!*"

# CHAPTER 12
## THE ABCD PATTERN

The ABCD trading pattern is a relative of the Elliot Waves in the sense that it is based on the fact that the market moves in an organized manner. In addition, it is one of the most profitable day trading strategies that you can find out there. Since the pattern is based on pure price action and follows market structure, it is a powerful leading indicator.

## STRUCTURE

The pattern uses impulse and corrective waves to predict the future of the market. The points named A, B, C, and D represent significant highs and lows in the market. When points A and B are joined, they form a wave known as a "leg." As such, the pattern is made up of legs AB, BC, and CD, where AB and CD are impulse waves, and BC is a corrective wave. AB and CD should be parallel to each other. We predict the future of the market by placing trades at the end of leg CD and in the direction of BC.

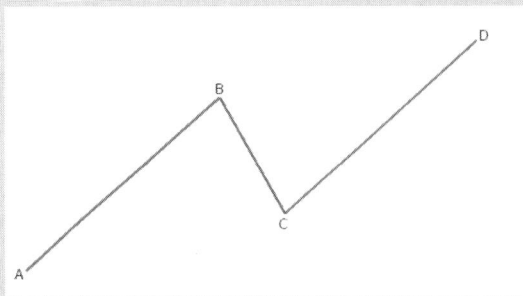

- Leg AB is equal to Leg CD in the "classic ABCD" pattern.

- Leg CD can extend by 127.2% or 161.8% in the "ABCD extension" pattern (more of the percentages later).

- The time it takes to form AB is the same it should take to form CD in the "Classic ABCD" pattern.

- Leg BC is the corrective wave and gives the direction of reversal after the completion of the leg CD.

Before we go any further into this pattern, we need to discuss an important tool that should be used alongside the pattern for better analysis. It is called the Fibonacci sequence tool.

## THE FIBONACCI SEQUENCE

The Fibonacci sequence is yet another important concept used in market analysis. It is very important in identifying the potential support and resistance areas, as well as the future movement of the market. It utilizes a little bit of mathematics to explain that everything in nature has a pattern known as the golden ratio that can be identified and used to explain things. For instance, the golden ratio can be used to count the number of veins in a leaf or the bones in a human being. We will not go too much into the mathematical derivations, as they are not very important to our lesson.

### Retracement Levels

The Fibonacci uses what we call retracement and extension levels to analyze the market. Retracement levels are the points in the market where a trend will pull back (correct) from the main trend before resuming the overall direction. In short, retracement levels can tell us how far waves 2 and 4 in the Elliot wave will go with more accuracy. In the ABCD pattern, these levels will tell us how far leg BC will move in proportion to leg AB.

The Fibonacci retracement levels are denoted as 0.236 (23.6%), 0.382 (38.2%), 0.500 (50%), and 0.764 (76.4%). You will understand them better when we draw them in the charts.

### Extension Levels

On the other hand, extension levels tell us how far the market will move in relation to a previous leg in the past. In the ABCD pattern, for example, we can predict how far led CD will move in relation to leg AB. As we stated in the structure of the ABCD pattern, in some cases, leg CD can be 127.2% or 161.8% longer than leg AB. The Fibonacci tool will help to identify these extensions.

The Fibonacci extension levels are 0 (0%), 0.382 (38.2%), 0.618 (61.8%), 1.000 (100%), 1.382 (138.2%), and 1.618 (161.8%).

### Using the Fibonacci Tool

To use the Fibonacci tool, you first need to identify some swing highs and swing lows in the market. A swing high is a point in the market that has at least 2 Lower-Highs on either side. In short, there should be a dominant candle and two or more lower-highs on its right and left sides. A swing low is the opposite of a swing high. It is a candlestick that has 2 higher-lows on either side.

To plot the Fibonacci levels, you use the Fibonacci Retracement tool found on the top-right side of your MT5 platform. It looks like this:

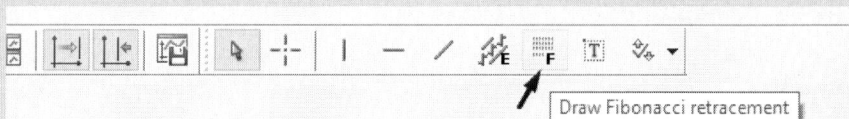

Draw Fibonacci retracement

## Plotting Retracement Levels

Remember that a retracement level means the points where the price might reverse (correct) from the main trend before resuming the general trend.

In an uptrend, you need to identify the most recent swing high and the most recent swing low. Choose the Fibonacci tool, click it, drag it from the swing high up to the swing low, and then release it. It will draw the retracement levels for you like below:

As you can see, after drawing the Fibonacci retracements in the uptrend market, the price pulled back and reached the 61.8% level, where it found support and went back to the main trend.

To plot the retracements during a downtrend, you need to use the Fibonacci tool and click on the most recent swing low and drag it up to the most recent swing high. Your chart will look like this:

From the image, you can see how the downtrend reversed up to the 38.2% and 23.6% levels before it resumed its initial main direction. Clearly, Fibonacci levels can be used as support and resistance points.

### Plotting Extension Levels

Fibonacci extension levels are plotted the same as the retracement levels. However, you need to tweak your tool a little by manually adding the extension levels that you want. To do so, attach the tool to your desired chat. Then double-click on the diagonal line in the tool to highlight it. Some three small squares will appear on the line. Next, right-click on any of the dots then go to "Properties" > "Levels." Find the level described as "100."

Now, you need to edit the number below 100. Double-click inside the first box below the 100, edit it to 138.2 and then change the level on the left side of it to 1.382. Click and edit the box below the 138.2, and edit it to 161.8. Also, edit the level to its right to 1.618. You can add or remove levels as desired. Click "OK," and the new levels will show up in your charts.

The extension levels are used in taking profits since they show the area where the market might move before slowing down or reversing. Here is a chart showing an extension level in a downtrend:

In the above image, you can see how the price went down after the retracement move. If a trader had placed their take-profit levels at either the 138.2 or 161.8% levels, they would have made their profits. You can also see how the two extension levels held the price for some time. Please note that these lines were plotted before the price had formed, yet the market respected them when it got to them. That is the magic of the Fibonacci tool!

Now, let us go back to the ABCD Pattern, and see how it is combined with the Fibonacci tool for the best results.

## CLASSIC ABCD PATTERN

The classic bullish ABCD pattern looks like the following image:

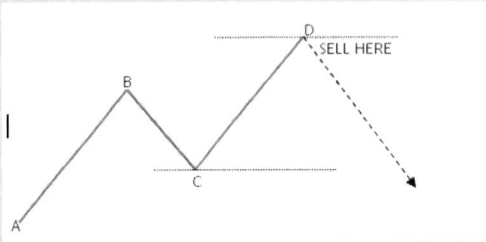

a) Classic bearish ABCD          b) Classic bullish ABCD

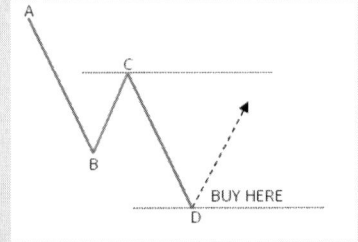

## In the above images:

- The length of AB is equal to the length of the leg CD

- The time it takes to form AB is the same it takes to form CD

- Point C should not go near point A. Similarly, point D should not be near point C. In short, you should have clear swing points indicating a good trend.

- The leg BC should retrace to 127.2% or 161.8% of BC. To plot this, since we have an uptrend, the Fibonacci would be drawn from point B (swing high) up to point A (swing low). Then as the market unfolded, it would bounce off C (retracement level) and continue to create leg CD. Once the trader is sure that the classic ABCD has been completed, they can enter a sell trade at point D (reversal into a downtrend).

## EXTENDED ABCD PATTERN

An extended ABCD pattern is different from the classic ABCD pattern in that the leg CD can be longer than leg AB by between 127.2% and 161.8%. Also, the time that it takes to form CD can extend by the same percentages. This pattern should look something like this:

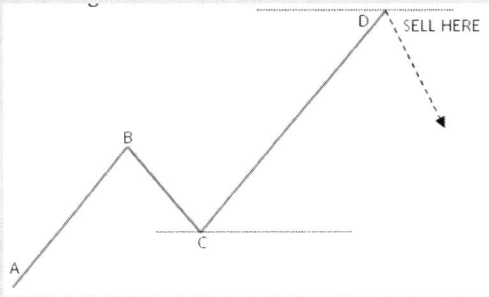

a) Extended bearish ABCD          b) Extended bullish ABCD

Here are two examples of the ABCD pattern in the charts.

Extended bearish ABCD pattern

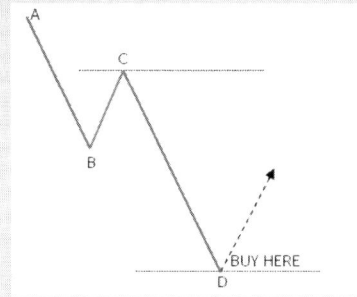

*Classic bullish ABCD pattern*

## Trading with the ABCD Pattern

You can add some of the other tools like support & resistance to your ABCD pattern trading style to improve the accuracy of the turning points. The stronger a zone is, the more likely that your leg is accurate. Fibonacci levels also work well when combined with support & resistance zones. Confluence at turning points or entry points can be increased by utilizing the knowledge of candlestick formations or a few indicators. However, be careful not to have too many tools in your charts as this can lead to analysis paralysis.

You must always keep in mind that no trading strategy is foolproof. You might have the best analysis and find the most promising trade signals, but still, the market might ignore and oppose you. Therefore, to be safe from excess losses, make sure to always have a protective stop-loss order immediately after you place a trade. The ABCD pattern makes stop-loss placement very easy. You need to identify a zone below or above point D and place it there. The First Take-Profit Level can be placed at the level of C. You can have a Second Take-Profit Level at point A or where your Fibonacci extension level coincides with strong support or resistance level.

## SUMMARY

How did you find this lesson? Was it as engaging and informative as I felt when it was first taught to me? I hope that you found it that way.

As always, I will emphasize two things: first, you have the freedom to choose which tools work for you. My objective here was to show you the best tools for day trading so that you can choose one or two or all of them! Second, put in as much practice time as you can with these strategies. Some of them, like the Elliot Waves and the ABCD pattern, require a lot of time to form. Therefore, exercise patience and do not be disappointed if a pattern fails, or it takes too long to give you a signal. Eventually, you will start seeing the importance of only taking the best trade signals and leaving the rest.

# CHAPTER 13
## RISK MANAGEMENT

Now that you are a qualified trader, you will come across people who will tell you that day trading is gambling. I used to get angry or disappointed when I was told the same. After some thoughtful consideration, I realized that they were right and wrong at the same time. They were right because the trading industry benefits the big players more than the retail speculators. Just like in all sorts of gambling, the casinos always win. The part of them being wrong is that it depends on the approaches that individual traders apply when fighting with the big boys, and this is where the aspect of risk management comes in.

Risk management is simply the aspect of controlling risks and ensuring that you have the edge over the market. Concisely, you need to install measures that will not only improve your winning but also ensure that your losses are insignificant. Remember that in the trading industry, losses are part and parcel of the process. However, your losses must be kept at a minimum so that in the long run, your portfolio will always be in profits. In my many years at trading, I have come to conclude that many traders who end up losing and quitting are those who ignore risk management.

Below are some of the ways that I have learned over the years that can help you in managing your risks and always being on the winning side.

## FOLLOW THE TREND

I have repeated this concept more than enough times within the book. Use your learned knowledge of identifying market swing highs and lows to know where the trend is heading. Build more confluence on matters of market direction by using indicators like the Moving Average or the OBV. Opposing the overall trend is suicidal.

## USE A STOP-LOSS

A stop-loss controls how much you are willing to risk for each trade. First of all, never trade without a stop-loss! Second, know where to place the stop-loss so that it is neither too close nor too far from your entry. A small stop-loss distance might be hit too soon, while a huge stop-loss distance can lead to excess losses.

## USE PROPER RISK TO REWARD

The risk to reward ratio is the best risk management approach to keep you in profits. It makes use of the stop-loss and take-profit orders collectively. The idea of this approach is to place your take-profit levels at least two times further than the stop-loss. In short, if your stop-loss distance is 20 pips, place your take-profit level at least 40 pips away.

You should consider the risk to reward ratio before entering any trade. Look at your tools of analysis such as support & resistance, Fibonacci, ABCD legs, and Elliot Waves to see which trades have a better risk to reward potential. If a trade has a 1:1 ratio (equal stop-loss and take-profit distance), consider ignoring it. Take only the trades that have a 1:2 or 1:3 risk to reward ratio only. Are you wondering why?

The concept is simple: if you place a 1:3 trade and it wins, it would take three losing trades (stop-loss is hit) to lose all the profit that you made. As such, even if you won only 3 out of every 5 trades that you made, you would still be in profit.

## USE CORRECT POSITION SIZING

Position sizing refers to how much of your capital you will risk at a go. In general, we always advise that each trade should not risk more than 2% of your trading capital. This is to say that if you have $200 in your trading account, your stop-loss should not risk more than $4. It would take 50 losses to lose all your $200. Do you get it?

Now, assume that you risked $20 per trade. You would only have to lose ten times, and your account would be wiped clean. Therefore, keep the position size very small.

## USE MINIMAL LEVERAGE

Leverage is known as the double-edged sword in on-line trading since it can bring a trade a lot of profit in a short time or take away as much money in a similar duration. Leverage allows you to borrow more money from your broker and place more or bigger trades. To be safe, use minimal leverage so that your risk is insignificant. When you have a leverage of 1,000, it means that for every dollar that you have, the broker can let you borrow 1,000 times more money. If you place a trade with such high leverage, it will take a few seconds before your account got wiped. Use minimal leverage that will allow you to risk less than 2% of your trading capital per trade.

## AVOID OVERTRADING

Trading is addictive; do not say you were never warned! Loving your job is an awesome feeling, but when it becomes addictive, then there is a problem. Try to control your trading time so that you are not always on the charts. Just like a typical job, fix the best time to be trading. Conduct a little research on the market that you are going to be trading and find out the best time to trade. In most cases, the best trading occurs when the majority of traders are active since there are enough volatility and volume for good trends to occur. Lastly, once you meet your daily trading targets, end your trading day and wait for another day.

## CONTROL YOUR EMOTIONS

The last and very important risk management trick is to take full charge of your emotions. The markets are controlled by human psychology; as such, you can gain an advantage in your trading by understanding how the markets work. This book has taught you enough of that. At a personal level, there are three types of emotions that you must keep in check for you to be successful at day trading:

- **Fear**

We can agree on the fact that trading is a risky career since it involves putting money on the line. Therefore, at some point in your trading, especially when you first start trading with a real account, you might be afraid of placing trades. This is normal, but you should not allow it to control your trading activity since it can lead to missed trading opportunities.

The reason you have been taught several of the best trading strategies in existence is for you to be able to place your trades with confidence. If you conduct accurate analysis and implement the right risk management principles, then you should have nothing to worry about your trades.

- **Overconfidence**

You should also manage the level of confidence that you have. Too much confidence might make you forget that the market is ruthless and does not obey anyone. When you forget the rules, you might end up taking premature signals, relying on automated systems, overriding proper position sizing, and generally exposing yourself to more risks.

Be confident, but keep the protective rules at your fingertips.

- **Greed**

Once you start raking in dollars, which I assure you that you will, do not be greedy. Overconfidence can lead to greed. You might find yourself risking too much of your account, placing a lot of trades, overtrading, and increasing your leverage in pursuit of more dollars. This might work for a short time, but eventually, a single silly mistake will place you on the bad side of the market, and that might leave you with deep psychological wounds and an empty wallet. Who wants that?

Risk management is as important to your trading as the strategy. You might have the best strategy in the world, but without proper risk management, you will end up with losses. Every profession in the world has its own rules that govern the safety and experience of the workers. Online trading is no different; you must utilize risk management. Put in as many of these concepts as you can, and you will find that trading is very easy. In addition, risk management cuts off the gambling aspect of trading.

# >> CHAPTER 14 <<
## CREATING YOUR TRADING PLAN

Our final chapter is dedicated to helping you to wrap everything up in a single package and boost your organization as a day trader. A serious trader needs a trading plan. This is more of a personal trading constitution that defines every aspect of your trading life. It defines why you are a trader and how you should trade at all times. The trading plan acts as a checklist that must be fulfilled before pressing the buy or sell button.

There is no definite template for a trading plan because each trader records what they feel is helpful to the trading. However, this does not make the trading plan optional; it is a must! In addition, it must be written down and accorded the respect that a constitution demands.

Here are some of the elements to include in a trading plan.

### WHY ARE YOU A TRADER?

The first component in your trading plan should be about yourself. You need to have clear motivation as to why you want to be a trader. Is it financial freedom? Do you love freelancing? Do bosses scare you? Whatever your motivation might be, list it down, as it will help to keep you going even during tough times.

## WHAT WILL YOU BE TRADING?

You must be very specific on the market and financial instruments that you will be trading. If you decide to trade stocks, binary options, futures, cryptocurrency, or forex, list it down. Narrow your definition further and list the specific instruments that you will be trading within your chosen market. For example, if you will be trading cryptocurrency, will you go for Bitcoin or Ethereum?

## HOW WILL YOU EVALUATE YOURSELF?

Every business needs to evaluate its performance and know whether it is making profits or losses. Similarly, you need to come up with some ways to tell whether you are growing or not. You can decide to conduct your evaluation after a number of trades or after certain durations.

## DEFINE YOUR TRADING STRATEGY

You should list all the components in your trading strategy and ensure that you adhere to them before executing any trades. List the way that you will be conducting your analysis from the analysis stage to the time you enter a trade. If you use indicators, define them, and explain how you will use them.

Do not forget to include stop-loss and take-profits.

## WHEN WILL YOU TRADE?

A trader must be orderly enough to know when they will be at their trading desk or not. If you decide to work in the morning or when specific markets are opening, then list that in your trading plan. Make sure that you are not on the charts at a time when the plan says that you should be elsewhere.

## HOW MUCH WILL YOU INVEST?

By the time you decide to deposit money with a broker so you can go live, you should have known how much money you can afford to use in trading. Initially, only invest what you can afford to lose without losing your mind. You can grow your capital as your experience expands.

Position sizing should also come here. You must decide how much money to risk per trade. Make sure you adhere to the money management rules that you come up with, no matter how appealing a trading setup looks.

## WHO WILL BE YOUR BROKER?

The choice of broker that you go for is crucial to your trading success. Conduct proper research on the best broker to work with. Some qualities of a good broker include:

- They are regulated by a relevant monetary body.

- They offer all the instruments that you need to trade.

- They are cheap in terms of commissions and other charges.

- They are reputable in all aspects.

- They are accessible any time you need them.

## WHAT ARE YOUR STRENGTHS AND WEAKNESSES?

Finally, you must evaluate yourself and see which of your traits make you a better trader and which ones limit your potential. Identifying your strengths will keep you motivated, and you will pay more attention to your stronger side. On the other hand, identifying your weaknesses will allow you to know what needs some improvement. You will become a better trader as you work on more of your limitations.

These are just some of the elements that you can in-clude in your trading plan. You can add more as you please, as long as they add value to your trading career. The most important thing, however, is that you follow the rules in your constitution to the end. If you only compose it and stop at that, it will be as good as seeing a good trade setup and letting it go. One day, when you are a successful trader, you will look back at this chap-ter and be proud that you began creating your trading plan the very moment you realized that this is the last page in your book :)

# >> CONCLUSION <<

Thank you for making it through the end of *Day Trading*. Let us hope it was engaging and informative while providing you with all the know-how that you need to achieve success in your day trading goals.

This book was composed in the best way to ensure you enjoyed studying online trading, which many people find too complicated. It brought together many years of experience and condensed the most useful knowledge to make anyone successful in trading the markets. We might say a lot, but the most important thing is that you end up a profitable trader without suffering as most traders do.

The next step is to start practicing all these concepts. Trading is a practical profession, and your success is highly determined by how much experience you have garnered. Therefore, put all the lessons in the book to practice in your MT5. You will internalize them and find that using them to spot winning trades is not only easy but also enjoyable. As you practice some more, you will settle on the best ones to be used in your daily trading life.

Finally, if you found this book useful in any way, I would appreciate it if you could recommend it to other people, as well as give it a review on Amazon. Thank you in advance for your consideration.

I wish you the very best as you start your successful day trading career. Thanks again!

# SWING TRADING
# STRATEGIES

A Beginner's Guide to the Stock Market. How to Apply Technical Analysis and Become a Swing Trader with Powerful Strategies to Trade Options, Stocks, Forex, Crypto, and ETFs

## MARK SWING

# >> INTRODUCTION <<

Thank you for picking this book out of the many books that have been written about Swing Trading on the Stock market. Swing trading is one of the favorite modes of trading as compared to day trading and position trading since it is steady and easy to grasp as well, especially for beginners. In the first chapter of this book, we discuss the basics of Swing Trading and the differences among the three forms of trading. The strategies that you can use when swing trading are also discussed in detail in the same chapter.

As you progress further into the book, you will read more on the different tools of trading that we can employ; such as platforms for swing trading, financial instruments necessary, and how to assess the risk associated with each trade. The information about trading psychology and how to maintain and update a trading journal is crucial to you as a trader; because you will need to have this information to finally trade.

The book also covers the basics of trading that include the strategies such as how to stop loss on trades and how to enter and exit the positions in order to maximize the profit that you can earn from a trade. In order to help you make these trades, we have covered extensively the major aspects of analysis every trader must employ. The Fundamental analysis is covered in its own chapter explaining what the trader needs to be on the lookout for in order to make the right decisions on the open positions they have already. The technical analysis, touching on the patterns, indicators, and Candlesticks evaluation covered in this book will help you in planning your day as a trader.

Finally, we have covered the different principles that every Swing Trader should adhere to in their daily planning of how to trade in the markets. The processes and analysis that are present in this book can be applied across markets such as the Forex, Stock Markets, or futures and options trading. You have made the first step in successful trading by downloading this book, enjoy as you read on.

Feel free to recommend it to your colleagues or fellow trader and if it is not too much to ask, please leave us a review on Amazon.

# CHAPTER 1
## SWING TRADING

There are three different types of trading in the world of Forex Markets and Stock exchange. These three trading methodologies are classified according to the period that the trade is open for. The long-term type of trading that can go for months or even years depending on the patience of traders is known as position trading. The traders who open their trades in the morning as the markets open and close when the markets close are known as day traders. These traders do not go to bed with any positions open and it includes traders such as the scalpers. The third type of traders are those who engage in swing trading, they do not open positions that are going to last for a very long time, and nor do they open trades that will last a short time. Usually, their positions are open for a few days, and the longest goes for a few weeks. We will focus more on this type of trader in this book since we want to tap into the steady profits they often take home regularly.

## DAY TRADING VS. SWING TRADING

Day trading, just as the name suggests, is about making many trades in a day. The day trader has to do technical analysis and check the positions every day. Their main intention is to make small profits on a number of trades while minimizing their losses. They open positions in the morning and close them all by closing hours.

The major limitation in day trading is the number of losses that day traders suffer when they begin trading. If one is not disciplined, they may end up borrowing money through margined trades and losing it leaving them in a huge debt.

The losses they make are because they compete against market professionals with hedge funds and millions to spend, giving them exclusive trading advantages. The key differences between day trading and swing trading are the lifestyles, likes and preferences, skills, and capital of the trader. A day trader has to be available full time and be passionate about his trading so that he can make a profit; while a swing trader can open a position and let it run for days while holding another job and making steady profits.

The second difference is day traders usually base their analysis on the technical side while swing traders have to utilize both the fundamental and technical analysis on their charts. Day trading involves risk-taking; the swing of the market is rarely on their side and they incur huge losses. Swing traders do not take on such great risks because their positions are pen throughout a period.

The vitality of day trading requires one to have control over their emotions so that they don't lose money and their discipline. Swing trading, on the other hand, is not as intense as day trading. Day traders expect their profits to be very little because their trading time frames are small. Swing trading assures the trader of a steadier and larger profit potential because their trading time frame is greater.

Day trading requires watching the number of trades opened in a day. You have to ensure that you open and

close it within the working hours of the day. Incidental-
ly, the more positions you trade, the higher your chances of losses. Swing trading doesn't need you to trade
on a daily basis. Usually, positions are open for two to
three weeks. They, therefore, encompass the breakaway gaps that price hits, earning them greater profits.
In money management, day trading gives a ratio of 1:4.
This means that a trader with 200k in capital can trade
financial instruments worth 800k during the day. Bear
in mind the more money you trade, the higher your
amount of losses.

Swing trading, on the other hand, gives a ratio of 1:2,
meaning the same trader, with 200k in capital can only trade 400k over the period they choose to trade. In
this case though, as a caution to both, traders should
not use the margin or have too much money invest-
ed in one position. They should also utilize a stop-loss
order to mitigate their risks and minimize their losses and always remember to pull some money out of
the markets and into their wallets. If you are a patient
trader, then swing trading is the perfect methodology for you. You can gain a lot from following a stock
trend. Day traders will receive instant gratification
and see their performance on a day-to-day basis. In
the closing hours, you can tell how much you won or
how much you lost.

In conclusion, neither trading strategy is better than
the other; it only depends on the trader's opinion and
answers to the following questions:

1. Why are you trading?

2. What is the amount of your initial capital?

3. How much risk are you willing to bear?

4. Do you like the adrenaline?

If you answer these questions honestly and go through this subtopic again, you will make your decision on what is best for you. If you still can't make up your mind, try a trading simulator to test both approaches so that you can be sure which strategy is best for you before you go live in the market.

# CHAPTER 2
## TRADING BASICS

The financial market draws together millions of individuals to trade a broad range of financial instruments around the globe. Being the most significant industry, some multiple securities or tools can be traded and used to plug in a significant quantity of profit from price changes. Forex plants up as the first trading tool or item for most traders who are just beginning to enter into trading. This has to do with the comparatively simple retail forex trading.

Being an extremely leveraged commodity and having a decentralized market allows it simple for the ordinary Joe to move money and begin trading to a forex broker. However, you can trade many products when it comes to the financial markets. Frequently, traders may have learned of ETFs, stocks, bonds, mutual funds, trading options, futures, among others.

In this chapter, the reader will get to understand the financial instruments vital for swing trading. The reader will also know some of the factors considered in the quest for a financial instrument usable in swing trading. Some of the most common trading instruments will be mentioned as well, with pointers on how people lose money and the amount needed to jump into the swing trading bandwagon.

## WHAT IS A FINANCIAL INSTRUMENT TO TRADE

A financial instrument is a monetary agreement that can be traded and resolved between two sides. The agreement reflects one party's asset (the customer) and the other party's economic liability (the vendor). An asset class relates to the type of commodities, stocks, derivatives, bonds, or Forex that a financial instrument uses.

Two classes of financial instruments can be divided: complex and non-complex.

**Non-Complex:** Complex financial instruments involve a thorough understanding to be effective when trading with traders. Derivatives are the most frequently traded complicated financial instruments. These may be CFDs, agreements for the future, and options. Various derivatives have distinct advantages. CFDs, for instance, are great for hedging. Since they are complicated economic tools, traders must get to know each derived product's nuances before beginning to trade them.

**Complex**: Without a great deal of expert expertise, non-complex financial instruments can be traded. They only need an initial investment in some instances, and then someone else, like a fund manager, makes investments on your behalf. Non-complex financial instruments include securities or equity, debt securities, and certain kinds of investment funds. Equity securities apply to commercial stocks, while debt securities relate to commercial and government bonds. Debt bonds can also apply to desired inventory and bonds types—such as collateralized equity commitments. Hedge funds and mutual funds are included in the investment funds. These are all tools that allow shareholders to distribute their cash under a fund manager professional: the fund manager. Typically, on behalf of shareholders, the fund manager will create equity choices.

## Factors to Consider When Selecting a Financial Instrument in Swing Trading

Volatility relates to economic security's capacity to increase significantly and decline. Therefore, volatility is a two-edged sword that can simultaneously be both a gift and a curse. High volatility appears to benefit traders who understand what they are doing as it enables them to produce numerous earnings. In moments of elevated volatility, however, a tiny error tends to accumulate casualties much faster.

1. **Information Availability:** In order to have a lucrative trading life providing safety, a free stream of data is essential. From time to time, news impacts rates, this way you should only trade when you have easily accessible news or data.

2. **Liquidity:** Relates to the facility at any specified moment to buy and sell a financial instrument. Instruments with elevated liquidity concentrations appear to be simple to trade as you can easily join and leave a situation.

3. **Low Costs of Transaction:** An economic tool with small transaction costs is perfect as it enables one to produce optimum yields on any particular trade. Brokers pay various trading charges for various financial instruments.

## Top Five Financial Instruments

### I. FOREX

As the world's biggest foreign exchange market, there are also some of the finest financial instruments that can be traded on a regular basis. The industry speaks for an ordinary weekly quantity of over $4 trillion. Due to their comparative stabilization, Forex tools are some of the finest to trade-in portion. The reality that these tools are accessible 24 hours a day also leaves them perfect for trade, regardless of jurisdiction, at any specified moment of the day.

One can use many economic tools. As much as retail forex traders often use foreign currency alternatives as an instrument for hedging, companies are more inclined to use alternatives, swaps, and other more complex derivatives to satisfy their specific hedging requirements.

Spot operations, futures, stocks, swaps, and forwards are some of the popular financial instruments used in Forex.

- **Spot Transaction**

A spot transaction is an arrangement at the present exchange rate to purchase or sell a currency. In other phrases, it is an easy currency exchange for another currency. It is usually resolved within two business days from the start of trading and involves a money swap rather than creating a longer-term agreement. At the moment of the agreement, the currencies are swapped at the spot rate. The spot rate constantly fluctuates as currency valuation shifts up and down in line with potential requirements. Spot operations do not require an instant deposit or settlement, normally setting the settlement date on the second business day after the deadline of trade. The deadline for trading is the deadline you plan to create the exchange.

The two-day duration gives traders sufficient opportunities to validate the contract and organize the processing and debiting and crediting of bank documents necessary. Interest in the pre-fixed operation is not included. Spot operations hold a heavy danger because they do not provide security against unfavorable exchange rate changes between purchasing a deal and buying/selling the foreign currency. Currency traders use spot operations to create earnings, purchasing small and distributing large, in the same manner as equity or commodity traders.

- **Options**

A currency option is comparable to a futures contract because, at some potential stage at the moment, it involves fixed currency exchange. A currency option provides the owner with the right, but not the duty, to either purchase from the choice writer or distribute a specified amount of one currency at a fixed exchange rate to the offer writer (in a swap for another currency).

The types of alternatives may be American or European. The choice can be practiced at any stage before the accepted expiry in an American-style choice. Only on the exercise date can the European options be exercised, not before. The option holder pays the option writer a premium for the option. The customer will waste the payment if the choice is not exercisable. Options safeguard the owner from the danger of exchange rate unfavorable modifications.

- **Swap**

In a swap agreement, one currency is swapped for a defined duration. The deal is overturned when the initial quantities are exchanged at a defined potential deadline. The two transactions take place at distinct prices of return. The swap cost is determined by the distinction between the two exchange rates. Swaps have different stages of maturity.

- **Futures**

A futures contract is a form of a forward contract with a predetermined quantity of cash, maturity, and deposit rate. A futures contract is an agreement to purchase or sell a currency at a price determined by the buyer and seller in a designated future month. They are standardized on futures exchanges and traded. Usually, a potential operation takes place within three months. Currency futures are always cited against the U.S. dollar in numbers of currency significance.

- **Forwards**

Forward operations require not less than three days ago to purchase or exchange foreign currency for payment and at predetermined exchange rates. In short, at a particular time and a particular exchange rate, a buyer and seller agree to trade currency regardless of what the exchange rate is when the transaction actually takes place. It is also possible to arrange a forward contract up to a year in advance.

The trader is shielded from currency changes for the agreement period by logging in a particular exchange rate. Forward contracts are not uniform, and on exchanges, they are not traded. This sort of financial instrument allows the trader to bring the benefit of presently favorable exchange rates in the future and to safeguard the trader against the danger of volatility of the exchange rate.

As they prefer to deliver elevated liquidity, Forex tools are also perfect for short-term day trading. They also arrive with elevated volatility rates that make it simple for traders to take benefit of short-term cost fluctuations. Traders should always prevent invasive currency pairs, however, because they lack the liquidity that is so much needed. Brokers often appear to charge large quantities of distribution on such currency pairs, which leaves it difficult for tiny cost motions to produce optimum yields.

## II. STOCK INDEX

The stock index reflects the importance of a set of one-nation stocks and demonstrates that specific stock index's general, present, and historical efficiency. Economists, leaders, and commentators can use stock indices to know the performance of financial markets and businesses in those sectors. A stock index could reflect the economy of the output country or the stock market of the whole world. S&P 500 is one of the finest inventory index economic tools. The index contains certain fee stocks taking into account the inventory of the biggest U.S. firms.

The S&P 500 is a diverse financial instrument, including stocks of up to 500 firms. That is why index performance acts as a good indicator of movement on the wider U.S. stock market. It is an optimal financial instrument because the index speaks for about a third of the worth of the full U.S. stock market. High liquidity rates, as well as volatility, implies that it can be easily traced.

## THE THREE MAJOR STOCK INDICES

Worldwide stock market indexes are strong indices for markets that are international and country-specific. In the United States, the press and shareholders' three most widely accepted indexes are the S&P 500, Dow Jones Industrial Average, and Nasdaq Composite.

### 1. Dow Jones Industrial Average

The second-oldest and best-known stock market index is the Dow Jones Industrial Average (DJIA). Its ownership is by Dow Jones & Company and controls the weekly cost motions on the NASDAQ and the New York Stock Exchange of 30 major American businesses. It is commonly regarded as a proxy for the overall circumstances of the market and even for the U.S. economy itself. Today, the parts of the DJIA are selected from all main economic sectors, except the transport and utility industries.

DJIA element stocks are not continuous; because of certain non-quantitative requirements, fresh entries and deletions are produced from moment to moment. Only firms are regarded for incorporation with a significant development history and broad investor concern.

DJIA is a price-weighted index, meaning that stocks with higher stock rates are assigned higher index weight. Instead of using an average number of stocks as division, as is done on an arithmetic average, a special divisor divides the sum of the component stock prices. The aim of this continuously adapted Dow divisor is to balance out the impacts of stock splits; dividends earned or commercial spinoffs; this enables a coherent index to keep the Dow from being affected by one-time occurrences. The outcome is that the DJIA is only influenced by stock price modifications, and stocks with a greater share price have a greater effect on the activities of the Dow.

## 2. NASDAQ Index

NASDAQ Composite Index is an inventory of all stocks traded on the NASDAQ stock exchange, weighted by market capitalization. Most shareholders understand that NASDAQ is the basis on which stocks of technology are traded. Hearing the finishing cost of the Nasdaq Composite Index published in the financial press or as the portion of the afternoon media is very prevalent because it is such a broad business stock.

Nasdaq Composite Index utilizes a weighting methodology for market capitalization. The value of the index is equal to the total value of each of the constituent securities' share weights, multiplied by the last price of each security. This number is then adapted by separating by an average divisor, which scales the significance for publishing reasons to a more suitable estimate. The index is continually calculated throughout the day of trading, but it is recorded once per second, with the ultimate verified score being published at 4:16 p.m. Every business day.

The calculation of two variants of the Nasdaq Composite Index is a price return index and a matrix of total return. The total return index involves money dividends being reinvested on their corresponding ex-dates of dividends. Both variants of the index include money transfers that are non-dividend. Index eligibility conditions are assessed year-round. Safety that does not fulfill the criteria of registration may be withdrawn at any moment, generally at its last selling cost.

## 3. S&P 500

S&P 500 is a stock market index that monitors 500 big-cap U.S. corporations' shares. It reflects the efficiency of the stock market by recording the hazards and yields of the largest firms. Investors use it as the general industry benchmark, which is likened to all other assets. The S&P 500 monitors in its ranking the company's business capitalization. Market cap is the complete valuation of all inventory holdings published by a business. It is calculated by multiplying the stock price amount of stocks sold.

Commission chooses the 500 corporations of each index depending on their liquidity, volume, and sector. In March, June, September, and December, it balances the index annually. To be able to qualify for the index, a company must:

- Have at least $1.6 million in market cap

- Should reside in the U.S.

- Should avail 50% of their stock to the public

- Have positive earnings in 4 consecutive quarters

- The price of its stock must be at least $1 per share

- File an annual 10-K report

- Have 50% of its revenues and fixed assets in the U.S.

Although one cannot invest in S&P, with an S&P Index fund, you can replicate its efficiency. You could purchase stock shares in the S&P 500 as well. Be ready to weigh them according to the market cap in your inventory, as the S&P does. The S&P 500 should be used as a major financial measure of how well the U.S. industry does. If shareholders trust the economy, they will purchase stocks. Some specialists believe that the stock market can forecast in about six months what the well-informed shareholders think the economy will do.

You should also monitor overseas economies as the S&P 500 only estimates U.S. shares. This involves developing economies such as China and India. In addition, keeping 10 percent of your commodity assets, like gold, is nice. When inventory rates fall, they appear to retain importance longer.

You should also follow the bond market after the S&P 500. When inventory rates rise, the price of bonds decreases. There are many distinct bond types. Tax bonds, corporate bonds, and municipal bonds are included. Bonds provide some of the liquidity that lubricates the U.S. economy.

The S&P 500 has larger shares than the Industrial Average of Dow Jones. The Dow is tracking the share price of 30 firms best representing their sectors. It is market capitalization represents nearly a quarter of the U.S. stock market. The Dow is the world's most cited business index. The S&P 500 has fewer shares related to technology than the NASDAQ. The NASDAQ also involves private-owned corporate stocks. All these stock indices appear to work together despite these variations. You will know how well the stock market is doing if you concentrate on one.

## III. EQUITIES

Other exceptional financial instruments, in addition to stock indices, are individual equities. Instead of gaining more exposure through indices, individual stocks of companies can be traded. Stock trading allows one to enjoy ownership of a company depending on the number of shares one buys. Because of the high levels of liquidity and volatility they come with, stocks of some of the biggest companies are some of the best for a day trade.

In part, stocks are popular financial tools because they come with high liquidity levels. Volatility and trading volumes, tend to vary on a daily, giving traders the opportunity to benefit from the slightest movements in prices. It is essential to take note of the things affecting stock prices when trading equities. Earnings that come out every three months are top on the list. Earnings have an impact on the share price as they act as an indicator of a company's financial health and long prospects. On investors looking at data, a stock price could essentially rise and extrapolate it to indicate the value of the company will rise with time.

The stock ratings of the analyst also affect the price of the share in one way or another. Analysts perform in-depth business analysis and therefore provide insight to traders on how they should trade. Industry news tends to affect the price of individual stocks with a domino effect.

## IV. COMMODITIES

Liquid commodities in the form of gold, crude oil, and silver pave the way for individuals to trade the financial market. As a financial instrument, commodities are a means of method provision if one wishes to diversify from stock indices and equities. One can purchase and exchange different kinds of commodities through exchange futures contracts. Such financial instruments are classified into five main categories: livestock and meat commodities, energy, precious metals, and industrial metals.

Delivery and request powers force rates on the commodities market. In this situation, a reduced supply of a specified commodity would lead to greater rates most of the moment, particularly on heavy demand. Gold is the most traded financial instrument in the commodity industry as it is viewed by traders as a means of conveying importance reliably and reliably.

In addition, professional traders switch to precious metals to hedge against elevated inflation or devaluation during phases of currency. Crude is another common economic tool as variations in oil yields (from reservoirs around the globe) affect rates enabling traders to benefit from cost modifications.

Agricultural products and grains tend to be extremely volatile and suitable for summer trading. Most of the time, population growth, as well as limited agricultural supply offer opportunities as they trigger price fluctuations.

## V. BONDS

Exchange-Traded Funds (ETFs), also known as bonds, are investment funds aimed at tracking the efficiency of indicators, commodities, or bonds in the industry in question. Some traders purchase ETFs instead of trading equities or indices as they create trade-like stocks. ETFs can be purchased and marginally distributed (as their value fluctuates), throughout a meeting of trading. They also provide higher diversification, and since they monitor only the efficiency of the fundamental indicators, there is a decreased danger.

Government treasuries serve as one of the best financial instruments given their safety net when it comes to exposure to risks. When it goes to yields as treasuries also recognized as bonds, no other financial instrument arrives with a promise. For this purpose, as some of the finest equity instruments for income-focused companies, they have persisted in bearing the trial of moments.

## HOW MOST PEOPLE LOSE MONEY

1. **Lack of Basic Know-How:** I have never taken the time to understand the fundamentals. The cause traders miss cash is because they forgot to know the correct foundations of how the stock market operates in their struggle to get trading. Get to know the stock market, some trading methods, and get plenty of paper trading exercises. Any information that you acquire will make your likelihood of achievement better.

2. **Lack of Savings:** Do not need to have a huge deposit to begin trading, contrary to a common faith. However, as your business expands, you need to be clever about what you are doing with your cash. If you burn your income every moment you create cash, you will never enhance your business place. You will be home to ground zero if you gain $8,000 on trade and immediately break it down. Smart traders see the large image and save a nice part of their earnings to enhance their situation gradually. They can boost their

assets. This usually matches their increasing skills as traders beautifully. These tiny victories gradually start to match up over time.

3. **Lack of Proper Research:** the process of creating a trade requires pure time, study, and preparation into a trade can extend hours, days, or even decades of surveillance and monitoring. Trading is a play of figures, and using previous data to create choices for the future is one of the keys to achievement. Looking at how it took place in the past, you can start doing business from a location of greater safety and trust. Prospective businesses and scanning the industry with an instrument are essential. This study will often disclose data that will assist you to identify whether or not at this specific moment a specific trade is a good idea.

4. **Lack of Proper Guidance:** Courses on daytime and/ or a mentor are key to assisting fresh traders to succeed. Classes can assist fresh traders in discovering not only the foundations but also experiencing distinct techniques of trading, which can assist them to create a range from which to start forging their own distinctive fashion. Another major is a mentor.

5. **Lack of a Trading Journal:** As you develop as a trader, you will advance through many techniques that function, and some that do not function. Just as much as you believe you understand precisely what is going on, only time can tell. By entering every trading day, including what you have done, how you feel, and the outcomes, you will receive a strong understanding of the techniques and procedures that really serve your profession. This will allow you to concentrate on what works and reject what is not.

6. **Fear of Failure:** A prevalent occurrence as to why traders are losing cash is that they are too scared to

make a loss. They are so afraid to lose cash that they follow only trades and deals that bring minimal danger. Although you should never be dangerous, you will have to move out a little bit of your comfort zone. To see benefits, you must embrace a certain amount of danger—or at least become familiar with it. The stock market is intrinsic in risk. One of the strongest methods to mitigate this, however, is to teach yourself and study extensively. This is the distinction between danger and calculated danger, and you can be more confident in your trade.

7. **Complacence:** This is never a stage where learning stops when you are a trader. You always need to be at the tip of your toes. For example, with a certain method, Joe, the trader becomes relaxed and just starts doing it, not holding a record of how the industry is moving. He becomes careless about their studies and screening is not so cautious. He is bound to start losing cash after a while. Complacency is a prevalent justification for losing cash to traders. You will probably start wasting over the moment when you stagnate as a trader. Never become idle in your studies, and never suppose that anything could land as a sure bet. Approach each trade as though it were your first, and look at it from every angle.

## HOW MUCH MONEY DO YOU NEED TO BE A SWING TRADER

How much money you are going to need depends on the approach you are using, which then influences how much you are going to profit through trade and the magnitude of your situation. To become an inventory swing trader, there is no minimum capital requirement. Day traders are required to keep a balance of $25,000 in their account, but this is not a swing trader's requirement. Just make sure that you do not wind up trading a bunch during the day. Otherwise, you will be susceptible to this minimum. Therefore, the resources you need are linked to your location magnitude, asset value, and trade danger.

Strategies for swing trading differ, yet controlling risk is one thing effective swing traders do. To determine how much money you will need to trade, first determine how much danger you are prepared to take on each trade (in cases of stored assets) as it impacts the magnitude of your properties. You can trade marginally as well. Stock market swing traders can leverage up to two occasions, which implies you can buy up to $20,000 worth of inventory if you invest $10,000. Account danger is always focused on loaned assets and not the quantity of leverage.

When it comes to reality, I think it is because they simply do not have enough cash that most swing traders and day traders struggle with. The unfortunate reality is that the majority of fresh traders are under-capitalized. After all, we have already found economies to be tough. Moreover, if you are trying to earn a living without enough cash, it is expected of you to lose your little piece. Swing traders are advised to rely on a single trade of less than 2 percent of account assets—even 1 percent or less.

You should begin swinging trading stocks with at least $5,000 to $10,000 as a fundamental thumb law. If you drop below these balances, you may wind up paying too much for each trade, as long as we risk at least $100 for each trade.

# CHAPTER 3

## NECESSARY TOOLS FOR SWING TRADING

Based on their price charts, technical traders create trade choices. Every technical trader is a bit distinct but can group the approaches they use into a few wide categories. There are mainly traders of indicators, price action traders, and traders using indicators and price action. Where fundamentalists are able to monitor economic reports and annual reports, technical traders depend on indicators to assist in market interpretation. The objective of using indicators is to define possibilities for trading. A moving average crossover, for instance, often predicts a shift in trend. Applying the moving average indicator to a price graph in this example enables traders to define regions where the trend may alter.

In this chapter, we will look into trading indicators and the different wheels of motion they are responsible for turning, moving average indicators, stochastics, and parabolic SAR.

### WHAT ARE TRADING INDICATORS

Indicators are technical analysis tools with a mathematical basis that is used by investors and traders to predict future patterns and trends and to analyze the past. The indicator indicates mathematical formula visual representation and cost inputs. An indicator will often not show more than what is noticeable to a qualified chart viewer or trader simply by evaluating the price graph (or quantity) without any indices.

Because a price graph has so much to analyze, an indicator helps to simplify it. Indicators have become so alluring to fresh traders due to this. Rather than studying how to define a price graph trend, they are trying to discover an indicator that will determine their trend and trend reversals. For traders to study, there is an increasing amount of technical indices accessible, including those in the public domain, such as a moving average or stochastic oscillator, as well as proprietary indicators that are commercially accessible. Moreover, with the help of a skilled programmer, many traders create their own distinctive indices. To suit the need of the traders, most indicators come with user-defined variables that give the opportunity to have key inputs.

### Examples of Trading Indicators

Four major types exist volume, momentum, trend, and volatility. Volume indices inform you how much volume changes over time, how many bitcoin units are purchasable and sold over time. This is helpful because the quantity provides an indication of how powerful the change is when the price changes. Bullish elevated volume movements are more probable to be maintainable than low volume movements. Trade quantity is a very significant trading element. It is usable in verifying or degrading a continuation or shift in the direction of a stock, for instance. There are also many indicators depending on quantity.

Indicators of momentum inform you how powerful the trend is and can tell you if there will be a reversal. They can be helpful in selecting the top and bottom prices. The Relative Strength Index (RSI), Stochastic and Average Directional Index (ADX) indicators are examples of momentum indicators. Momentum traders concentrate on large volume stocks or assets that move considerably in one direction.

Trend indicators intend to demonstrate the trend or direction of the asset they are trading to traders and investors. An asset's trend can either be downward (bearish trend), sideways (no definite direction) or upward (bullish trend). Sometimes people refer to them as oscillators because they tend to move like a wave between elevated and low values. Examples of some of the trend indicators are parabolic SAR, moving averages, linear regression, MACD, and forecast oscillator.

Indicators of volatility inform you how much price changes over a specified period. Volatility is a very significant component of the industry, and there is no way to make cash without it. Furthermore, to make a profit, the price has to go up. Trading volatility is so important that you can find multiple indicators to measure it or use it to generate signals. There is high volatility when the price moves up and down rapidly over a short timeframe. If the price moves slowly, we can consider that, the volatility is low. Envelopes, Bollinger bands, volatility channels indicator, true average range, projection oscillation, and volatility Chaikin are some of the volatility indicators available to traders. Usually, the measure of volatility occurs using the standard deviation. However, there are many other measures of the volatility of assets.

### Choosing the Right Indicator

What kind of indicator a trader uses to create a strategy depends on what kind of approach they intend to build. This refers to the style of trading and the level of tolerance of risks. A trader looking for long-term movements with big revenues could concentrate on a trend-following approach and thus use a trend-following indicator like a moving average. A trader interested in tiny movements with regular tiny profits may be more interested in a volatility-based approach.

Traders do have the choice to buy "black box" trading systems. They are proprietary strategies that are commercially accessible. A benefit of buying these black-box schemes is that all the research and theoretical backtesting is there for the trader. The disadvantage is that the user is not able to know what is happening behind the scenes, as the methodology is not reveal-able and the user is often unable to create any customization to represent his business style.

## HOW TO USE TECHNICAL INDICATORS TO DEVELOP STRATEGIES

There are many distinct categories of instruments for technical trading. Traders often use various indicators to create a policy, although when using more than one, distinct kinds of indicators are suggestable. Using three distinct indicators of the same sort, such as momentum, results in multiple counting of the same data, which is 'multicollinearity' in statistical talk. One must avoid multicollinearity since it produces redundant results and can make other variables appear less important. It is vital for traders to consider mixing up a little, they should pick an indicator from each of the categories and use them concurrently, maybe use one trend indicator and use a momentum indicator in their analysis.

For instance, a moving average approach could use a momentum indicator to confirm the validity of the trading signal. One indicator of momentum is the RSI, comparing the average price change of progressing periods with the average price change of decreasing periods. The RSI, like other technical indices, has user-defined variable inputs, including determining which concentrations will represent circumstances of overbuying and overselling. Consequently, the RSI is essential to verify any signals produced by the moving average. Opposing signals might show a less credible signal and avoid the trade.

Each combination of indicators and indicators needs research to determine the most appropriate imple-mentation for the style and tolerance of the trader. One benefit of quantifying trading laws into a strategy is that it enables traders to apply the approach to his-torical information to assess how the approach would have been accomplished in the past, a method known as backtesting. This does not, of course, ensure future outcomes, but it can definitely assist in developing lu-crative trade policy.

Regardless of which indicators come to play, a plan must accurately define how the results are to undergo interpretation and what action is viable. Indicators are instruments used by traders to develop policies; they do not build on their own trading signals. Any ambigu-ity may cause difficulty.

## BENEFITS AND DOWNSIDES OF INDICATOR TRAD-ING

Each indicator has a weakness; something that makes it likely to deliver trade signals at the incorrect mo-ment, or fail to deliver a trade signal at the right mo-ment. Study math below it if you use an indicator. That way, the vulnerabilities are workable. You should also not place your bet too much on the time an indicator said you were doing something that led to your victory or defeat, but also pay close attention to the times it did not give you signals to join or leave a trade.

Another indicator drawback is that they typically only show what is happening on the price chart, but visually differently. Price action traders feel that indices are redundant and unnecessary, as they can only provide data that price (and quantity) graphs still provide. As indicators are calculated on a volume basis (or price, or both), they tend to lag in what the price is doing.

The topmost downside of indicators is that they may appear to be deceivingly easy to use on the outside yet traders have no idea what is happening behind the sense of the indicator. Therefore, they do not have an idea when the indicator will show a bad or good signal.

The primary advantage of indices is that price movements are simplified. New traders may discover an indicator's easy motions simpler to interpret than the price chart's complicated gyrations. Note that in this situation "simpler" does not imply more lucrative. However, indicators are an outstanding instrument to learn how to detect weakness or strength in the price when a trend is weakening.

This may be difficult for a new trader to evaluate on a price chart, but they are prompted by subtle changes that they have not yet trained themselves to see on the price chart with the help of some indicators.

## MOVING AVERAGE INDICATORS

In technical analysis, moving averages serve as the most common indicators. In addition, the most important indicator may be the moving average itself, as it is the cornerstone of countless others, like the Moving Average Convergence Divergence. Filtering the "noise" from random short-term price fluctuations makes the price action smooth. It follows the trend, or lags because it is run by prices of the past. A common application of the moving averages is to determine the direction of a trend and the level of support or resistance.

The Simple Moving Average (SMA) and the Exponential Moving Average (EMA) are the most basic and commonly used moving averages. The SMA is the simple security average over a specified number of periods while
the EMA gives the more recent prices greater weight.

### The Simple Moving Average

The SMA is a basic price average over the timeframe
specified. For example, if one plots a 50-period SMA on
a chart, the previous 50 closing price is added and divided by the number of periods (50) to determine what
the current SMA value should be. To form a line, a series
of different points are put together. To make it easier
to see a security's price trend, a simple moving average smooths out volatility. This implies that if the simple moving average adds up, the cost of the security
increases. If it points down, it implies the cost of the
security is falling. The longer the moving average time
frame, the smoother the moving average.

The median lengths of common movements are 10,
20, 50, 100, and 200. Depending on the time horizon of
the trader, these distances are implementable to any
graph time interval (one minute, daily, weekly, etc.). The
time interval or duration you select for a moving average also referred to as the "look back era," can play a
major part in how efficient it is.

### Limitations of the Simple Moving Average

Whether or not more emphasis is place-able on the
latest days of the era or on more remote information
is uncertain. Many traders think that fresh information
will better represent the present pattern with which
safety moves; while others think the trend will be bi-
ased by privileging certain dates than others. The SMA
may, therefore, depend too strongly on obsolete information as it handles the effect of the 10th or 200th day
just as much as the first or second day.

Likewise, SMA depends entirely on historical information. Many individuals think exchanges are effective—that is, present market prices already represent all the data accessible. If markets are effective, the use of historical information should teach us nothing about the potential asset pricing path.

## THE EXPONENTIAL MOVING AVERAGE

An exponential moving average (EMA) is a form of moving average that puts more weight and importance on the latest information points. Together with other indices, EMAs are frequently used to verify important business movements and assess their legitimacy. The EMA is more relevant to traders trading intraday and fast-moving companies. Traders often use EMAs to identify a trading bias.

## THE DIFFERENCES

The main distinction between a simple moving average and an exponential moving average is the sensitivity of the information used in its calculation. More specifically, the EMA provides the latest sales with a greater weighting, while the SMA assigns an equivalent weighting to all items. The two scores are comparable because they are understood in the same way and are both frequently used by technical traders to smooth changes in prices.

Because EMAs position a greater weighting on recent information than on earlier information, they are more sensitive to recent cost modifications than SMAs are, making EMAs outcomes more timely and explaining why the EMA is the favored average among many traders.

## MOVING AVERAGE INDICATORS EXAMPLES

### 1. Bollinger Band

A technical indicator for Bollinger Band ® has usually put two standard deviations away from an easy average of movement. Overall, a transition to the upper group indicates that the asset becomes overbought, while a step close to the reduced group indicates that the asset becomes oversold. As standard deviation is usable as a statistical volatility measure, this indicator adapts to market conditions.

### 2. Moving Average Convergence Divergence (MACD)

Traders use the moving average convergence divergence (MACD) to monitor the two moving averages' connection. Its calculation is done by removing an exponential moving average of 26 days from an exponential moving average of 12 days.

The short-term median is above the long-term median when the MACD is favorable. This is a sign of the momentum upwards. The momentum is decreasing this symbol when the short-term average is below the long-term median. There will also be many traders watching for a shift above or below the zero lines. A step above zero is a buying signal, whereas a cross below zero is a selling signal.

### 3. Signal Line

For any type of information that shifts commonly, moving averages are developable. A moving average of a technical indicator such as the MACD can even be taken. When the indicator value passes the signal line, buy signals are produced, while brief waves are produced from a circle below the signal row.

## PARABOLIC SAR

In an effort to create prospective purchase and sell signals, the Parabolic Stop and Reverse (SAR) index incorporates price and moment elements. The Parabolic SAR is an efficient instrument for determining where to position stop-loss instructions. The indicator, an invention of the well-known technician J. Welles Wilder Jr., is easily implementable to a trading strategy, allowing a trader to determine where to place stop orders.

One of the most intriguing elements of this measure is that it implies that at any stage in time, a trader is fully engaged in a situation. For this purpose, those who create trading systems and traders who always want to have cash at the job in the economy are particularly interested. The parabolic SAR indicator represents itself as a sequence of points positioned either above or below the cost (based on the momentum of the asset) on the graph of an asset. When the flow of the asset is upward, a small point is put below the cost, whereas a point is positioned above the cost when the flow is reversed.

In economies with a constant pattern, the parabolic SAR works better. The parabolic SAR appears to whip back and forth in a wide range of industries, producing fake trading hints. In order to achieve a more precise evaluation of the intensity of the current pattern, Wilder suggested increasing the parabolic SAR by using the average directional index (ADX) speed indicator. Candlestick models or shifting statistics may also be a consideration for traders. For instance, cost dropping below a significant moving average is drawable as a distinct confirmation of a parabolic SAR selling message.

The indicator's primary benefit is that the marker will show that powerful pattern during a powerful wave, maintaining the trader in the fashion movement. The indicator also provides an escape when a step against the pattern is taking place, which could indicate a change. Sometimes this finishes up being a nice departure as the market reverses; sometimes, it is not a great departure because the value starts moving in the path of the trend again immediately.

The main drawback of the indicator is that during sideways business circumstances, it will provide little analytical understanding or excellent trade hints. The indicator will constantly flip-flop above and below the cost because there is no tendency current. It is suggested that traders study to define the pattern—by studying cost intervention or using another indicator—so that trades can be avoided when there is no pattern and trades can bring place when there is a tendency.

## STOCHASTICS

A stochastic oscillator is an indication of momentum contrasting a specific opening cost of safety to a spectrum of its rates over a certain span of a moment. The oscillator's sensitivity to business motions is reduce-able by changing that time span or by getting a changing outcome median. It produces over-bought and over-sold trade messages, using a limit value variety of 0-100. Stochastic oscillator mapping usually comprises of two rows: one that reflects the oscillator's real significance for each meeting and one that reflects its simple moving average of three days. Because cost is believed to follow momentum, it is regarded that the junction of these two rows is a hint that a change may be in the works, as it implies a big change in momentum from day today.

Range-bound is the stochastic oscillator, implying it is always between 0 and 100. This allows it a helpful marker of circumstances that are overbought and over-sold. In the overbought spectrum, measurements over 80 receive traditional regard, and measurements below 20 are considered over-sold. These, however, are not always reflective of an anticipated inversion; very powerful developments for an expanded era can retain over-bought or over-sold circumstances. Instead, traders should search for hints about potential pattern shifts in the stochastic oscillator for modifications.

George Lane created the stochastic oscillator at the end of the 1950s. As Lane's design preference, the stochastic oscillator shows the location of a stock's closing price over a period of time, typically a 14-day period, in relation to the high and low price range of the stock. Lane has said in countless surveys that the stochastic oscillator does not follow cost, quantity, or anything like that. He points out that the oscillator is following the cost velocity or momentum. In surveys, Lane also shows that the momentum or velocity of a stock's value shifts before the value itself shifts.

Thus, when the index shows bullish or bearish divergences, the stochastic oscillator could be of use to foreshadow reversals. This message is the first trading message recognized by Lane, and possibly the most significant one.

### Fast Stochastics

The Stochastic Oscillator is an indication of momentum that indicates the closing position relative to the high-low spectrum over a fixed amount of times. The index may vary between 0 and 100. The holding cost continues to fall in an uptrend close to the high and in a downtrend close to the bottom. If the finishing cost slides back from either the large or the small, the momentum slows down. In wide trading distances or rapid shifting patterns, stochastics are most efficient.

### Slow Stochastics

The Slow Stochastic Oscillator is an indication of momentum that indicates the closing position parallel to the high-low spectrum over a fixed amount of phases. The index may vary between 0 and 100. The holding cost continues to fall in an uptrend close to the high and in a downtrend close to the bottom. If the finishing cost slides back from either the large or the small, the momentum slows down.

The main variance between fast and slow stochastics is that the fast stochastic is more susceptible to changes in the cost of the underlying security than the soft stochastic and will probably come in many exchange hints. However, you should first know what the stochastic momentum index is all about in order to comprehend this distinction.

### Limitations of Stochastics

The stochastic oscillator's main restriction is that fake waves have been found to be produced. That is when the indicator generates a trading signal, yet the price does not effectively go through, which can wind up being a winning trade. This can occur quite frequently in unstable business circumstances. One method to assist with this is to adopt the cost pattern as a buffer, where only if the measurements are in the same path as the pattern.

# CHAPTER 4

# FINANCIAL INSTRUMENTS FOR SWING TRADING

Swing trading is a very unique and interesting thing that more people are learning about simply for the benefits that they will have from learning how to do this. However, one of the most important things that you need to learn is the financial instruments that you're going to need to make this possible so that you can do this well. Swing trading combines fundamental analysis and technical analysis to catch price movements while avoiding idol times. The benefits that you can get from this type of trading are a more efficient use of higher returns and capital returns and the drawbacks are more volatility and higher commissions. Swing trading can be very difficult for the average retail trader and this is because the professional ones will, of course, have more information, more leverage, experience, and lower commissions.

However, they're also limited by the instruments that they're allowed to trade in the first place and the risk that they are capable of taking on is an issue as well. Knowledgeable traders can take advantage of these things to profit consistently in the marketplace so the first thing that you need to do is understand what financial instruments you need to make this a viable career for you.

The first thing that you should understand is the pre-market. The reason that this can be a financial instrument that you can use for yourself is that when you're able to understand it you'll be able to understand how early you need to get yourself going, a schedule that you'll need to put yourself on and finding the right instruments that you can use to benefit yourself before somebody else takes advantage of it. If you are a retail swing trader, then you should know that you will often begin your day as early as six in the morning. This is well before the opening bell. The time before the opening bell is actually crucial for getting an overall feel of the day's market and this is going to help you find potential trades, create a daily watchlist, and check up on existing positions. This is a very important financial instrument that you can use for yourself because if you don't understand the pre-market then you're not going to be able to do this properly.

Another thing that you can do for your benefit financially is to find potential trades. A trader needs to be able to scan for potential trades throughout the day and they also enter a position with a fundamental catalyst so that they can manage or exit positions. You can do this with the help of technical analysis. The first way to do this is through special opportunities that are found in SEC filings or in some cases you can even find it in the headline news.

Some opportunities that will outline what was talked about are the following:

- Bankruptcies

- Insider buying

- Takeovers

- Mergers

- Restructurings

- Acquisitions

Typically, these can be found by moderating such filings as the S-4 or 13D. This can easily be done with internet sites which will help send notifications as soon as filings are made, but you need to make sure that it's an actual SEC filing site and not a site pretending to be one. These types of opportunities usually carry a large amount of risk but they also deliver many rewards to those who can carefully research each opportunity and use the financial instruments to their benefit.

The other opportunity that you can use here is the sector base. These opportunities are found by analyzing the news or consulting a reputable financial information website and making sure that that is real as well. For example, if you want to see if an energy sector is hot all you would have to do is look for a popular energy exchange trading fund or scan the news. Traders are looking for higher risk and higher returns in some cases and they can choose to seek out more obscure things or more obscure sectors. They're often very much harder to analyze but they can also yield much greater returns for the trader.

Chart breaks are the third type of opportunity that is available to swing traders. These are usually stocks that are heavily traded and that are near a key support level or a key resistance level. In order to take advantage of this, the swing traders will look for different types of patterns so that they can be able to predict the breakdowns or breakouts such as triangles and channels. You should know however that charge breaks are only significant if there is sufficient enough interest in the stock.

These types of plays usually involve the swing trader buying after a breakout has occurred and then selling again very shortly thereafter at the next resistance level. A financial tool that you can use for yourself is the market overview. The first task of the day that you should be doing is to catch up on the latest news and development in the market, the quickest and easiest way to do this would be through your cable television network. CNBC or reputable websites such as MarketWatch are the most popular and accurate way to do this as well. To benefit from this, you need to keep an eye on three particular things:

1. The current holdings as the first ones that we will be mentioning. This means SEC filings and their earnings.

2. The sector sentiment means the growing sectors or the hot sectors. It also means the overall market sentiment which means the key economic reports, inflation, overseas trading, and things of that nature. If you are in the pre-market hours, then you should be checking the existing materials that are already there. Review the news to make sure that nothing material has happened to the stocks and this can be done by typing in a stock symbol into a news service. You'll need to see whether the files have made the Edgar database and if there is any material information that should be analyzed in order to determine how it's going to affect your current plan.

3. Making a watchlist is also important because you're going to be looking at your stocks daily. This means that this is a stock that has been a fundamental catalyst and has a shot at being a good trade for you.

Financial instruments are viewed as legal agreements that require one party to pay money, something else of value, or promise to pay under a stipulated condition to a counterparty in exchange for a payment of interest for the acquisition of certain rights, or premiums or an identification against risks.

It can be an actual document such as a stock or a long contract. It can even be something just like a certificate but increasingly these have been standardized and are stored in electronic book-entry systems as records and the parties to the contract are also recorded. An example of this would be the United States Treasury. It's stored electronically in a book-entry system and is maintained by the Federal Reserve.

## THE MOST COMMON FINANCIAL INSTRUMENTS THAT YOU CAN USE

- **Stocks.** Stocks are issued by companies to raise money from investors.

- **Checks.** Checks transfer money from the writer of the check to the payee or the receiver of the check. A bond. A bond is a financial instrument that will allow investors to lend money to the issuer of the bond for a stipulated amount of interest over a specified period.

Financial instruments can also be used by traders to do a number of different things including the next levels or interest rates. Or they speculate about future prices and things of that nature. The two parties of this kind of instrument are known as hedgers or speculators. Speculators look in the future or some other financial measure that may be a financial instrument that would yield a profit if they view that they think that the future would be correct. A hedger is someone who attempts to mitigate financial risk by buying or selling financial instruments whose value would be inversely varied with the hedged risk.

You also need to understand the difference between financial instruments whether it's derivatives or cash. The two main types of financial instruments that you can have are known as derivative instruments or cash instruments. A derivative instrument is also known as an instrument that you derive from value and today that means different things. Underlying assets or interest rates are examples of what we're talking about here. Cash instruments on the other hand are instruments that the market values directly. An example of this would be securities because they're readily transferable and deposits along with loans. Agreements between lender and borrower where they must agree on a transfer are also considered cash instruments.

You can also have financial instruments by asset class. This includes equity-based financial instruments and debt-based financial instruments. The difference between these two is that an equity-based financial instrument reflects the ownership of an issued entity. A debt-based instrument works like the loan that the investor made to the issuing entity.

Some of the most common examples of financial instruments can also include asset-backed security, which is where lenders pull the loans together before selling them to investors. As such, the lenders will receive a lump-sum payment immediately and then the investors receive payments of interest or principal from the underlying pool.

Funds include exchange-traded bonds, mutual funds, or real estate investment funds along with a long list of other funds. These funds buy other securities, earn interest, and capital gains which means your share price of the fund.

Currency trading is a tool to use as well. Currency trading is also done for capital gains but it can be used to earn interest as well. The swap is another financial tool that you can use for your benefit and it is an exchange of interest rate payments that are calculated as a percentage of a notional principal that will be paid at periodic intervals.

Other types of swaps that you can do are a currency swap or an interest rate swap. Another option to utilize is an exchange of money for protection against risk which would be insurance. Insurance contracts the promise to pay for a loss event in exchange for a premium.

Primitive securities are based on real assets or on the promise or performance of the issuer. A financial derivative which is another financial instrument is based on an underlying asset that could also consist of other financial instruments or benchmarks. This would include things like credit events, or stock indexes.

The value of any financial instrument depends on how much it is expected to pay but it is also dependent upon the likelihood of them getting paid in the first place or the present value of a payment. The reason that financial instruments are so sought-after is that they believe that they will have less risk but a higher value than other instruments that you can use. The present value of the payment would be determined by when the payment will be made so if you have a payment that you need to make a greater amount. The more time until payment the less of the value and security that they would have so that lowers the volume.

When you are selecting a financial instrument there are many different things that you will need to consider and if you're not able to learn about these things, you could be walking into a situation that's going to be unbeneficial for you instead of beneficial which has the exact opposite of what you want.

The first thing that you'll have to be aware of is called volatility.

This refers to the ability of financial security but more specifically refers to the ability to rise and fall sharply.

This is believed to be a double-edged sword because it can be a blessing and a curse at the same time. If this is high, it actually tends to work to the advantage of the traders who understand what they're doing because it allows them to generate profits multiple times. You can see how this would be a great thing for you. However, if you have even the smallest mistake in these times where this is high, your loss will accrue much faster and you can get yourself into situations you can't get out of. This is where it becomes dangerous and unhelpful. As such, this is something you should really understand before you dive into it headfirst.

The next thing that you'll have to be aware of is liquidity. Liquidity is what refers to the ability to buy and sell a financial instrument at any given time and how easy it is for you to be able to do so in the first place. If you have an instrument that has a high level of liquidity you will notice that it tends to be really easy to trade as you can enter and exit the position that you have with ease.

You also need to be able to have the availability of information. You will not be able to do this properly if you don't understand what it is you are doing in the first place and if you have no information with which to use to your advantage. So having that availability of information is going to be able to help you so much more than you even realize. The ability to be able to utilize the free flow of information is vital if you expect to have a profitable trading career. This is especially true if you're trading what is known as given security. The news will affect prices from time to time and you should only trade an instrument if that newsworthy information is readily available to you. If the news information is not readily available you won't be aware of the fact that materials can change, stocks can also change and so many factors affect them both. Many things can get changed and you would have no way of knowing this.

You shouldn't trade if you don't have information because you shouldn't put yourself in any situations that you might not be able to get out of. This can cause you problems as a trader.

Low transaction costs are important as well. A financial instrument like this will have a broker charging different trading fees for different situations financially. This particular tool is ideal because it allows you to get optimum returns on any given trade.

There are many different instruments that you can use when you're a trader and we've gone over many of them here. The foreign exchange market is the largest in the world and it comes with some of the best financial instruments that you can trade daily. Considering the 3 trillion average daily volume that this has, this would be something to learn to use to your benefit as well. The foreign exchange instruments are some of the best to trade in because of their relative stability and the instruments are available around the clock which also makes them in high demand. You should avoid the exotic currency pairs, however. This can be a bad move for you to make.

This is because the brokers charge exorbitant amounts of spread. This makes it hard to get returns on them.

Indices will highlight the performance of the country's economy or the entire world stock market. There are many financial instruments that you can use under this category and the index stocks that you need to take into consideration along with this.

In addition to the other things that we've mentioned above individual equity can be a financial tool for you to use as well. Instead of gaining greater exposure to other options, you can use the option to trade individual stocks of a company. This is what's known as stock trading. Stock trading will allow you to enjoy the ownership of a company depending on the number of shares that you buy for that company. Stocks are a popular investment because they come with high levels of liquidity but you should be aware that they also come with the things that you need to avoid like volatility and trading volumes. However, you can make both of those work well for you as well, which we have also mentioned above. You should also be aware that they vary on a daily basis which allows you to take advantage of the slightest price movement. This is obviously something that would be a benefit and a smart thing to look into as a trader because you can take advantage of the market and get opportunities that other traders will not have been made aware of as of yet.

Now that we have given you the information that you need to be a successful trader and to understand all the information that goes behind financial instruments and how you can use them to your benefit, you can take the information that you've learned in this chapter and learn which tools would be the best fit for you and which ones you should avoid for the time being or understand that they may cause more harm than good. Apply it to your trading and you should be successful. Remember, that there are many different tools that you have at your disposal with this career and you should use that to your advantage so you are able to push past others in the same field.

# CHAPTER 5
## FUNDAMENTAL ANALYSIS

Fundamental analysis is concerned with the well-being of the economy. The current progress of inflation, the interest rates, and balances of deficits among others are very important to fundamentalist analysts. They analyze the different political and economic situations of the countries to see the type of possible movements either short or long term the market is likely to make. Some of the factors fundamentalists consider are interest rates.

The Federal Reserves and the central banks look at the different economic indicators before they make the decisions on raising or lowering the interest rates in their respective countries. The rate of interest greatly influences the movements in the Forex markets. The higher the rate the lower the volume of trade and the contrary is also true.

## AVERAGING DOWN INCORRECTLY

Most people say that you shouldn't average down. The reality is that beginner traders should not average down. However, as you become more proficient or a lot better in trading, you become more successful in trading, there are certain situations that you may want to average down. This is because you put on a small tiny position and you prepared for a little bit of a pullback.

When you have this experience, and you see a potential for the stock to continue to sell up a little bit, further that you don't mind buying it a little bit at a lower price because you're positioning for that situation and you are preparing for that situation in those cases and situations averaging down is perfectly fine. However, if you know you have the world in your hands and you are ready to go, and the stock is against you, and you start averaging down, and you start using the leverage, and you start putting more and more money into a losing trade that is automatically a wrong approach. This is not a healthy way that you want to average down into position. This is meant for gurus and money managers. Remembers nobody knows when the stock is going to go bankrupt. Be prepared that if you are averaging down, you can do it at most twice if you are new. But if you have experience, you can work it out based on your strategies, maybe when the conditions are right, and you are prepared for them. You, therefore, need to catch yourself and save a position instead of losing it.

## USING EXCESSIVE LEVERAGE

You will always have this urge of trading more, especially if you are experiencing losing positions. You were maybe trying to trade options, or you are using the margins because you don't have enough money. Most people do worse when they are using leverages. They don't understand how these things work. Therefore, they don't understand options, as options are more complicated and you need to use more capital instances to make up those differences. You have to have the sock moving, especially if you are just buying puts or calls. Thus at the beginning using leverage like options and margins, they become worse off than just buying three or five shares of a specific stock. Remember, if you don't have enough money, you are trying to use leverage or margin to make that difference. You need to start slow get better and build some consistency before you use the leverage. Use the too available to make more money instead.

## GETTING EMOTIONALLY TIED TO A STOCK

Often some traders get attached to a specific stock, and this is due to the emotional ties to a particular product or company. Maybe this is based on what you saw on Twitter or social media platforms. You get emotionally tied perhaps because you use the product; thus you are involved with the company. You have a relationship, and you, therefore, make investment decisions with no clear mind. If this is what you are also using when it comes to stock, ask yourself how it would be if the stocks turn around or sell-off and you have no other plan in mind. You need to know that there have men many hundred successful companies that have failed over time. And you will realize that this is happening to many people. A lot of people put their money into specific equities, certain trading vehicles, or believing in individual companies, and eventually, those stocks go lower and lower and lower and never come back up. You should, therefore, not get so emotionally tied to a particular stock. Don't be bothered by what the stock sells; however, all you need to care for is if the stock is moving. Is it continuing to make a certain consistent return time and time again? How is it behaving, how is the price action? Is it stable? To answer this, you need to look at your trading plan. Do not get attached if it is not; it is not talking or walking the right way to your plans. Be out of the trade if it is not doing something sensible to you.

## NOT TAKING PROFITS INTO STRENGTHS

Most traders go into stock entirely and make the full profit once it reaches a specific number. You need to take profits slightly into depths as that stock continues running in your favor. This is because you never really know when that stock will pull back.  If an inventory is moving up, let us say two months, you continue making higher highs, it is fantastic and enjoyable to you. Take a little money off the table. Take maybe a quarter, half, a fifth, or a third off. Take that profit and put it back into your account and go ahead and do something with it elsewhere. Don't just allow the stock to continue to run higher and higher without taking any profit because the bigger the stretch, the longer that they keep stretching, the more likely it is going to have a pullback. Pullbacks are very healthy for stocks as they create new stock patterns, create new opportunities, and allow you to buy more shares from those profits that you took. The problem is that many traders get into a stock fully committed, and they don't make profits, and all of a sudden in one day the stock starts to go down even below their entry price. You need to note that the down days are much more violent, and one or two big down days can take one or two months' worth of gains. This is why it is crucial to take up money into strengths. You need not be scared of making up your profit. Yes, you do want your winners to run as long as possible, but you also need to know that not taking profits is just as bad as keeping them there.

## HOLDING ON TO LOSERS

The market will please some people and also annoy some people. I believe that you don't want to hold losers. Thus you need not be tied emotionally to a particular stock. When you bought a stock at $50, it goes to $75, it now starts to sell up, and it then goes to $70 the $65 and then to $55 and gets back to 50 dollars that you bought it and you still hope that it goes up? If you continue holding just a little bit longer it will continue to go lower to $40 a share or $30 a share, you are now going to a fastener, and you are starting to lose money in a big way. And now what people do is that they are at a loss and say that "well, I am just so deep into it I might as well keep holding on to it." This is a big problem as you are holding on to losers longer than you should, especially if you had a profitable stock or a profitable trade. You should NEVER let a winning business turn into a losing trade that's why you take profits into strength as mentioned earlier. Holding on to losers away too long is another huge mistake that you should avoid.

# CHAPTER 6
## TECHNICAL ANALYSIS

Technical analysis is considered a discipline of trading used to identify trading opportunities and evaluate investments by analyzing statistical trends. The trends are from trading activities, such as the movement and volume of price. Technical analysis focuses on the trading signals, patterns of the movement of prices, and other analytical charting tools. Traders can forecast price directions in the future by using a security's past price action, mainly through charts and indicators.

## CHARTING BASICS

### Candlesticks

Candlesticks are a form of price charts. They display the low and high prices, opening prices, and closing prices over a specific period.

A candlestick has four data points:

- Open

- Close

- High

- Low

The position of the open or close depends on whether

the candlestick is bullish or bearish. Bullish candlesticks have their open below the close, and bearish candlesticks have the open above the close. The shadows of the candlestick show the high and low of the day and their comparison to the open and close. The shape of a candlestick varies and has its basis on the relationship between the high and low prices, open price, and close price of the day.

Technical analysts can use candlesticks in determining when to enter a trade or exit it. This is because the candlesticks show the impact of investor sentiment on the prices of the security. They are suitable for trading liquid assets such as foreign exchange, stocks, and futures.

Candlesticks that are long and white or green indicate strong buying pressure. This shows that the price is bullish. Black or red candlesticks, which are long, indicate significant selling pressure. In this case, the price is bearish.

### CANDLESTICK PATTERNS

Candlestick patterns are useful in predicting the direction of the price. However, not all patterns are efficient. Their popularity was lowered when well-funded players deconstructed them. These players rely on speedy execution when trading against experienced investors together with fund managers who implement strategies from technical analysis. Though hedge fund managers reduce the reliability of candlesticks, there are reliable patterns that allow short-term and long-term opportunities. These patterns include:

- **Three-line strike.** It is a bullish reversal pattern. It contains three black candles which occur in a downtrend. Each of the three bars has a lower low than the prior candle and closes around the low of the intrabar. Though a fourth bar will open lower, it will reverse and close above the first candle's high. The opening print marks the fourth bar's low. This reversal tends to predict with an 84% accuracy rate.

- **Two black gapping.** After a notable top in the uptrend, this pattern appears. It is said to be a bearish pattern. It has a gap down, which leads to two black bars having lower lows. The pattern indicates a continuation in decline and perhaps a broader downtrend. It has a 68% accuracy rate and predicts lower prices.

- **Three black crows.** This is a bearish reversal pattern. It starts around a high of an upwards trend. It consists of three black bars having lower lows closing around the lows of the intrabar. It predicts the continuation of the descent. It has a 78% accuracy in predicting lower prices.

- **Evening star.** It is a bearish reversal pattern. It begins with a tall white bar. The bar increases the high of the uptrend. On the next bar, the market will gap higher but yields a narrow candlestick since buyers do not appear. The pattern is complete by a gap that goes down the third bar, predicting the continuation of the descent. It has a 72% accuracy and predicts lower prices.

- **Abandoned baby.** It is a bullish reversal pattern that occurs after a downtrend. It forms after several black candles. On the next bar, the market gaps are lower, but since there are no fresh sellers, it yields a small range of candlesticks with equal open and closing prices. The pattern is complete by a gap that is bullish along the third bar which can be a prediction that the recovery continues to higher highs. It has an accuracy rate of 70% and predicts higher prices.

## BASIC BULLISH AND BEARISH CANDLESTICKS

Two bullish principles have to be taken into consideration. The first is that bullish reversal patterns form within a downtrend. The second is that the patterns require bullish confirmation.

There are a few bullish candlestick patterns that have strong reversal signals:

- **The Hammer and Inverted Hammer.** The hammer is a signal that the stock is approaching the low in a downtrend. The candle's body will become short and have a lower shadow which is long. This signals the presence of sellers who during a trade tend to lower the price. However, buying pressure increases to ensure the trade ends on a high close. The Inverted Hammer will occur within a downtrend. It represents a potential reversal of a trend. It differs from the Hammer in that there is buying pressure indicated by a long upper shadow. Selling pressure comes after the initial buying pressure but it is not strong enough to lower the price below the opening price.

- **The Bullish Engulfing.** It is a reversal pattern that contains two candles. The second candle submerses the first one's real body. It occurs in a downtrend. It is a series of dark candles proceeded by a larger hollow one. On the pattern's second day, the price will open below the low of the previous day but will be pushed to a higher than the prior high by the buying pressure.

- **The Piercing Line.** It is also a reversal pattern that contains two candles. It occurs in downward trends. A white candle follows the first long black candle and will open lower as compared to the prior close. The buying pressure will then push the price up halfway or more into the black candle's real body.

- **The Morning Star.** It is a sign of a new beginning and it occurs in a downtrend. It is formed by three candles; one short candle (Doji) between a long black candle and a long white candle. The short candle and the black one, which is before it, do not overlap at any point. It shows that selling pressure from the prior day subsides. The white candle will overlap the black's body. It shows renewed buyer pressure and the beginning of a bullish reversal.

- **The Three white soldiers.** The pattern forms in a downtrend. It consists of three long white candles. The candles close higher each day. They open higher than previous opens and close around the day's high. It shows a steady increase in buying pressure.

A few important bearish candlestick patterns include:

- **Bearish Engulfing.** This pattern has two candles, a white one and a long black one. The black candle engulfs the white candle. After advancing, the black candle forms when the buying pressure results in the trade opening above the prior close. Sellers, however, step in and drive prices down after this opening gap. Selling becomes intense by the end of the session, causing prices to move lower than the previous close. This results in the black candle engulfing the body of the previous candle, creating a likely short-term reversal.

- **Evening Star.** It has three candlesticks; one white and long candle, a black or white small candle which gaps above the prior candle's body, and a long black candle. The white candle confirms the strength of buying pressure within an uptrend. When the second candle gaps up, it indicates residual buying pressure, but the advance slows afterward, possibly due to indecision or reversal of the trend. The small candle is a Doji, which increases the possibility of a reversal trend. The third candle confirms the bearish reversal.

Both bullish and bearish candlestick patterns require confirmations.

### Bar Charts

Bar charts show several bars over a period. Each bar shows the price movement over a specified time. Typically, each bar shows the open, high, low, and close prices (OHLC charts). However, it is adjustable to show high, low, and close (HLC charts). Technical analysis uses bar charts to monitor the performance of the price, which aids in the making of trading decisions.

Each bar in a bar chart has a vertical line that indicates the highest and lowest prices reached during that period. A small horizontal line marks the opening price. It is to the left side of the vertical line. The line on the right side of this vertical line marks the closing price. If the closing price is below the open price, the bar can be read since the price drops during the period. If it is above the opening price, the bar can be black or green. Color coding helps traders see trends and price movements easily.

The bar chart analyzed is up to traders and investors. Day traders would prefer 1-minute bar charts, while long-term investors may want weekly bar charts. This is dependent on the period they want to analyze.

There is a lot of information that traders utilize on a bar chart.

Long vertical bars show that there is a large difference between the low and the high of that period. It means volatility increases during the period. Short vertical bars mean there was little volatility.

If between the opening and close prices, the distance is large, it means that the price made a very significant move. If the closing price is significantly higher than the opening, it shows buyers were active, which may be an indication that more buying is forthcoming in future periods. If the close is closer to the open, it shows little conviction in the movement of the price.

Color-coding bar charts based on the rise and fall of the price provide information at a glance. Green or black bars usually represent an uptrend, while red bars represent downtrends and downward movements of the price.

It is advisable to use bar charts with other technical analysis indicators and tools.

### Price Action and Psychology

Price action is a description of the characteristics of the price movements of a security. It is a trading technique used by traders in reading the market and making trading decisions. These decisions are based on the actual movement of price, instead of technical indicators.

Psychological and behavioral interpretations are important aspects of price action trade. No two traders interpret price actions the same way. Each trader has their way of thinking, rules, and different understanding of the price actions.

Technical analysis tools are taken into account since the price action trading relates to recent data and past movements of prices. These tools include charts, price bands, trend lines, high and low swings, and technical levels.

Experienced traders who follow the price action trading employ several options for recognizing patterns, stopping losses, entry or exit points, and other related observations. Most of them have a two-step process:

- Identify a scenario such as breakouts or reversals.

- Identify opportunities within the scenario. Opportunities are subjective and vary among traders.

Price action trading is more suited for short or medium-term trades. By combining price history and technical analysis tools to identify trading opportunities, price action trading has a lot of support from traders in all markets.

Advantages of price action trading include:

- Self-defined strategies which offer flexibility to traders.

- Applicability to multiple classes of assets.

- Easy usage with any trading software.

- Traders feel in charge of their trades.

### *Gaps*

A gap is an area on the chart where the price of trade rises or falls from the close from the previous day with no trading happening in between.

Gaps usually occur when news or an event gets traders into the security. It results from the price opening significantly lower or higher than the closing price of the previous day. It may indicate the beginning of a new trend or the reversal of the previous one.

There are different types of gaps:

- **Breakaway gaps.** They occur at the end of a pattern's price and signal the beginning of a new trend. They appear when a price tests a level. The price gaps through the level and begins a new trend in the breakout's direction. These gaps are easy to spot. Once a trader spots them, they can join the new trend while it is still in the early stages.

- **Continuation gaps.** They occur in the middle of a pattern and are a sign of a rush of traders who think the price will continue in the same direction. During an uptrend, a bullish gap is a bullish continuation gap. If the trend is a downside, a bearish gap is a bearish continuation gap.

- **Exhaustion gaps.** They occur near the end of a pattern and are a sign of a final attempt to hit new lows or highs. During this time, the last of the traders join the trade, and with no one to continue supporting the trend, a reversal in price action follows an exhaustion gap.

- **Weekend gaps.** They specifically take place after weekends. They occur because trading does not take place during the weekend, but there are usually major announcements or events during the same weekends. As a result, a good number of trading orders accumulate before the weekend is over, and these orders do not meet counter orders. Traders then have to open positions for prices lower or higher than those seen on Friday.

One of the limitations of gaps is the inability of traders to distinguish between the different types of gaps. Misinterpretation of gaps could be disastrous as one misses the opportunity to buy or sell. This could weigh heavily on a trader's profits and losses.

### Fibonacci Retracement

Fibonacci retracement is a term used by technical analysts. It refers to the support areas or resistance areas of trade. Fibonacci retracement levels employ horizontal lines as an indication of likely support or resistance levels. Every level associates with percentage, where the percentage shows how much the price retraces from the previous move. The levels include 23.6%, 38.2%, 61.8% and 78.6%. 50% is not an official ratio but is still used.

The indicator does not have any formula for calculating it. When used to a chart, the user decides two points, and lines are then drawn with respect to percentages of the move.

The numbers of the Fibonacci retracement come from the Golden Ratio. Begin a sequence with 0 and 1. Add the two previous numbers and you will get a string of numbers:

0, 1, 1, 2, 3, 5, 8, 13, 21, 34, 55, 89, 144, 233, 377, 610, 987...

The Fibonacci retracement levels are derivatives of this sequence. Aside from the first few numbers, dividing a number by the next one will result in 0.618 or 61.8%. Dividing a number by the second one to its right will result in 0.383 or 38.2%. Aside from 50%, the basis of the ratios lies in the calculation involved with this number string.

The Golden Ratio, 0.618 or 1.618, can be found in the formation of galaxies, sunflowers, shells, architecture, and historical artifacts.

Fibonacci retracements are useful in placing entry points, determining stop loss, and setting price targets. An example; a trader sees a stock moving up and retraces to the 61.8% level, then it bounces again. The trader decides to buy because the bounce was at the Fibonacci level, with the trend being the longer uptrend. The trader could also set a stop loss at 78.6% or 100% level.

They are also used in other forms of technical analysis. These forms include Elliot Wave Theory and Gartley patterns.

Fibonacci levels are said to be static prices. The static nature allows the levels to be quickly and easily identified, which allows traders to anticipate and appropriately react to the testing of the price levels. The levels are points of inflection where there is an expectation of price action, whether it is rejection or a break. There is a difference between the Fibonacci retracement and the Fibonacci extension. The retracement applies percentages to a pullback, while the extension applies percentages to moves that are in the trending direction.

A limitation of the Fibonacci retracement is that there is no guarantee that the price stops at the support or resistance levels. It shows potential, not confirmation. Another limitation is that there are many levels that a price could reverse near any of the levels. Traders find it difficult to know which level is going to be fruitful in the current market.

## SWING TRADING INDICATORS

### *Support and Resistance levels*

Support is a price level where any downward trend is expected to stop because of excessive demand. As price decreases, demand increases, forming a support line. Meanwhile, zones of resistance arise because of a sell-off after the price increases.

Identifying a zone of support or resistance provides likely trade entry and exit points. This is because when a price arrives at the point of support/resistance, it'll do either of these things. It will bounce from the level, or it will violate the level, continuing with its direction, until the proceeding level.

Experienced traders tell stories of how certain levels of the price prevent traders from pushing the price in a certain direction. Resistance levels are known as ceilings because they prevent prices in the market from moving upwards. Support levels are known as floors because they prevent the price from being pushed downwards.

The static barrier that prevents prices from moving higher or lower is a popular form of support or resistance. The price, however, is in constant movement either upwards or downward, so it is possible to witness the barriers change with time. This is the reason why knowing trending and trend line concepts is important as you learn more about support and resistance.

When the market has an upward trend, resistance levels form when the action of price begins to slow down and pulls back to the trend line. This occurrence is a result of taking profit or, sometimes, near-term uncertainty. The resulting price undergoes a slight drop-off in stock price, or the plateau effect, and creates a short-term top.

When the market trend downwards, traders observe a series comprised of declining peaks. They attempt to join the peaks with a trend line. When the price nears the trend line, traders watch the trade to see if it encounters selling pressure. They consider entering a short position as this is where the price can be pushed downward.

The strength of support or resistance of a known level increases with more prices that fail to move beyond it. Technical traders use these levels to pick their entry or exit points since these are areas that represent prices that impact an asset's direction. They have confidence in the levels because the volume increases more, making it difficult for the traders to drive the price lower or higher.

Another characteristic of resistance or support is round numbers. An asset's price has a hard time going past a round figure price level; for example, $50. The majority of traders with little experience tend to buy or sell once the price is a whole number since they feel that the stock has a value at such levels. Retail investors and large investment banks, among other groups, set stop orders and target prices at round price levels. The round numbers act like strong price barriers because a lot of orders are placed at those specific levels, thus creating levels of support or resistance.

Sometimes, a support level becomes a resistance when a price tries to move up after it moved past the support level. The resistance level will become a support one when a price falls, after breaking the resistance level. Price charts allow traders to identify support and resistance areas. They also have clues regarding the levels' significance. They observe:

- **The number of touches.** The more a price touches a support/resistance area, the more important the level is perceived. When the price bounces off the level, traders take note and form their trading decisions based on the level.

- **Prior price move.** If the levels precede steep declines or advances, they are considered more significant.

- **Volume at certain price levels.** The support or resistance level is possibly stronger when more buying and selling occurs at those levels because traders will have the levels in mind and choose to reuse them.

- **Time.** When the levels are tested regularly over a long period, they become more significant.

Moving averages, extensions, and Fibonacci retracements can be interpreted as support and resistance indicators.

### Moving Averages

Moving average is a common indicator used by technical analysts. It filters the noise from short-term price fluctuations, smoothing out price action. Its basis is on previous prices, making it a trend following indicator.

The two most basic and common ones are the simple moving average (SMA), which is the simple average of a security over several periods, and the exponential moving average (EMA), which emphasizes mostly the recent prices.

The formula for the simple moving average is:

$$SMA = \frac{A_1 + A_2 + \cdots + A_n}{n}$$

Where A is the average in the nth period and n is the number of periods.

The formula for the exponential moving average is:

$$EMA_t = \left[V_t \times \left(\frac{s}{1+d}\right)\right] + EMA_y \times \left[1 - \left(\frac{s}{1+d}\right)\right]$$

Where EMAt is the EMA today, EMAy is the previous EMA, Vt is the value today, s is smoothing, and d is the number of days.

Moving averages tend to lag behind the current price as they have their basis on previous prices. The lag is usually long when the moving average period is long.

The length used of the moving average is dependent on the trader's objectives during a trade. Short-term trading uses shorter moving averages, while long-term investors prefer longer moving averages. The widely used moving averages are the 50-day and the 200-day MAs.

Moving averages convey significant trading signals when used alone or when there is a crossover between two averages. A rising moving average is an indication of uptrend security. A declining moving trend shows a downtrend security. Similarly, a bullish crossover confirms upward momentum and occurs when a short-term moving average crosses above a long-term one.

This is sometimes also known as a golden cross. Bearish crossover confirms downward momentum, occurring when the short-term moving average crosses below the long-term one. It is also referred to as a dead cross.

Moving averages are customizable indicators. The user is free to choose whichever timeframe is suitable to them when creating the average. The common timeframes, however, are 15, 20, 30, 50, 100, and 200 in terms of days. When a short time is used, the average is more sensitive to changes in price. A longer time period smooths out the average. The efficient way to know which timeframe works well for you is by experimenting with the periods until you find what you want.

Differences between the SMA and the EMA:

- SMA is calculated by simple arithmetic meanwhile EMA's calculations emphasize recent prices for it to be more receptive to new data.

- EMA responds quicker to the changing of prices as compared to the SMA since it has more lag.

- SMA identifies support and resistance levels more easily since they represent the true average of prices.

- EMA tends to turn before SMA when trends change direction.

Although there are differences between these two moving averages, none is necessarily better than the other.

Examples of the moving average indicators include the MACD and the Bollinger Bands®.

### *Relative Strength Index*
The RSI is a momentum indicator. It is used to measures recent price changes and carries out evaluations

of oversold and overbought conditions within a market. It displays as an oscillator; that is, a line graph moving within two extremes, and may read from 0 to 100. J. Welles Wilder Jr. developed the indicator and brought it to light in his 1978 book, New Concepts in Technical Trading.

The traditional interpretation of the RSI is, any value above 70 is an indication of an overvalued market, also known as overbought, while any value below 30 is an indication of an undervalued market, also called oversold.

The RSI has a two-part calculation process:

$$RSI_{step\ 1} = 100 - [\frac{100}{1 + \dfrac{average\ gain}{average\ loss}}]$$

The average gain/loss used is the average of the percentage gained or lost during the look-back period. The standard is using 14 periods to calculate the RSI value.

Once we get the 14 periods of data, we can calculate the second part of the formula:

$$RSI_{step\ 2} = 100 - [\frac{100}{1 + \dfrac{previous\ average\ gain * 13 + current\ gain}{previous\ average\ loss * 13 + current\ loss}}]$$

Using the above formulas, we calculate RSI where the RSI line and price chart are plotted next to each other.

The RSI rises and falls according to the increase of the size of positive closes or losses. An increase in positive closes leads to the rise of RSI, while an increase in losses results in a fall of RSI. After the second calculation smoothes the results, the RSI will be near either 100 or 0 in a market that is trending strongly.

To ensure the indicator's readings are understood properly, the primary trend of a stock is important. The

RSI has divergences. Bullish divergence happens when the RSI has an undervalued reading then a higher low which equals the corresponding lower lows. This will likely indicate bullish momentum that is rising. A break above the undervalued area could cause a long position. A bearish divergence happens when the RSI has an overvalued reading, then proceeded by a lower high which equals the higher highs of the price.

Swing rejection is a trading technique used to examine the RSI behavior as it re-emerges from an overbought or oversold area. A bullish swing rejection contains four areas:

- RSI falls into an undervalued area.

- RSI moves back over 30%.

- RSI forms another dip but does not cross back to the oversold area.

- RSI breaks its most recent high.

A bearish swing rejection mirrors the bullish one. It also contains four areas:

- RSI rises into the overvalued area.

- RSI moves back below 70%.

- RSI forms another high but does not cross back to the overbought area.

- RSI breaks its most recent low.

Andrew Cardwell developed another trading technique to go with the RSI, positive, and negative reversals. A positive reversal occurs when the RSI and security form lower lows and higher lows respectively. The lower low is not at the oversold area, but around 30-50%. A negative reversal occurs when the RSI and security form higher highs and lower highs respectively. The higher high is just below the overbought area. Positive and negative reversals place the price action first, then the indicator second. It challenges the way we think about momentum oscillators.

One limitation of the RSI is that it is most reliable when it comes to long-term trends. It is difficult to differentiate between true reversal signals and false alarms during a short-term trend. Another limitation is the RSI is less reliable outside oscillating markets.

### Bollinger Bands®

A Bollinger Band® is a tool used by technical analysts. They have two standard deviations which are line defined, both positive and negative, away from an SMA of the security's price. It is adjustable to suit the preference of the user. John Bollinger, a famous technical trader, developed and copyrighted Bollinger Bands®. Since standard deviation measures volatility, the bands widen when the market is more volatile and contract during less volatile periods.

To calculate Bollinger Bands®, find the SMA of the security, usually using a 20-day SMA. A 20-day SMA is the average of the closing prices from the first twenty days. This is the first data point. The next data point is the addition of the earliest price and price on the 21st day then finding the average, and so forth. Then obtain the standard deviation of the price of the security.

The formula is:

$$Upper\ Bollinger\ band = MA(TP, n) + m * \sigma[TP, n]$$

$$Lower\ Bollinger\ band = MA(TP, n) - m * \sigma[TP, n]$$

Where MA is the moving average; TP is the typical price which is the summation of the high, low, and close, divided by three ($\frac{high+low+close}{3}\frac{high+low+close}{3}$); n is the number of days in the period of smoothing, usually, twenty; m is the number of standard deviations, usually 2; and σ[TP,n] is the standard deviation over the last n periods of the typical price.

A good number of traders believe that the market is overbought, the closer the price moves to the upper band and oversold when the price is closer to the lower band.

The central concept of this indicator is the squeeze. A squeeze is the constricting of the moving average because the bands are close together. It signals a period of low volatility. Traders consider it to be a potential signal of an increase in volatility in the future and trading opportunities. Bands that are wider apart signal volatility decrease and might result in the exiting of a trade. However, it is important to note that these conditions are not signs for trading. The bands do not indicate the direction of the price or when a change will occur.

Approximately ninety percent of price action happens within the bands. A breakout below or above either band is a significant event. The breakout is, however, not a sign of trading. Breakouts do not provide clues to the direction of the price and are not a sign to buy or sell.

A major limitation of the Bollinger Bands® is that they cannot be used alone during trading. They are only indicators that provide information on the volatility of a price. John Bollinger suggested using the bands with non-correlated indicators which give more insight into the market signs directly.

### Parabolic Stop and Reversal

The parabolic SAR indicator determines the direction of the price of an asset. It is sometimes referred to as the stop and reversal system. It draws attention to the changing of the price's direction.

On a chart, the parabolic SAR appears either above or below the price bars, as a series of dots. A dot below the bar is a bullish sign. Consequently, a dot above the bar is a sign of bearish trends. When the dots change, it is an indication that a possible change in the direction of the price is underway.

An increase in prices results in the rise of the dots which slowly pick up speed and accelerate with the trend. As the trend develops, the SAR moves faster. The dots soon catch up with the price.

The indicator utilizes the most recent extreme price (EP), which is the highest and lowest, together with an accelerating factor (AF) to find where the dots will appear. Its calculation is:

$$uptrend\ PSAR = prior\ PSAR + prior\ AF(prior\ EF - prior\ PSAR)$$

$$downtrend\ PSAR = prior\ PSAR - prior\ AF(prior\ PSAR - prior\ EF)$$

Where EP is the lowest low for a downtrend and highest high for an uptrend and updated every time a new EP reaches, and AF is the default of 0.02. The AF increases by 0.02 every time a new EP reaches a maximum of 0.20.

The indicator also sets stop-loss orders. It does this in two ways:

- **It behaves as a trailing stop.** Instead of placing one-stop loss where the trade entered, be it below a long position or above a short position, the stop loss slow-ly raises for a long position, and lowers for a short po-sition, taking in any profits, using the parabolic SAR as a guide.

- **Acts as a time stop.** Traders use time stops because they enter a trade expecting certain moves to occur. If the moves do not occur and the trader's reason to initiate the trade is not relevant, they opt to exit the trade. The parabolic SAR incorporates time in its cal-culations to ensure trade is beneficial to the trader. If it does not move in the expected direction, the indi-cator suggests an exit point.

A potential buy signal by the parabolic SAR is when the price closes over the upper indicator. When the indi-cator moves below the price from above it, the trader may decide to buy in order to cover the short sell, then change direction, buy to go long.

A potential sell sign is when the price closes beneath the indicator. When the indicator moves above the price from below it, the trader stops and sells to exit the trade, then changes the direction and sells.

The parabolic SAR has one main advantage, among oth-er advantages. The indicator highlights occurring strong trends, assisting a trader to remain in the trend. The indi-cator also shows when there is a possible move against the current trend and gives the trader an exit option.

A disadvantage of the indicator is it does not provide good trade signals or analytical insight during sideways market conditions. The indicator will constantly move below and above the price because there is no trend.

### Stochastic

George C. Lane developed the Stochastic indicator in the 50s. It is a momentum indicator. It gives the position of the recent closing price in relation to the previous range of highs and lows. The indicator takes a comparison of the previous trade range and the closing price to measure momentum over a certain period.

It follows the momentum and speed of the price, instead of the price and volume of the underlying currency. It is considered a leading indicator because it changes its direction before the price in the trend. The stochastic indicator identifies bullish divergence and bearish divergence, together with overbought and oversold prices.

To draw the indicator on a chart, we use two lines: the indicator, %K, and a signal line, %D. The signal line represents a three-day simple MA of the indicator. When the lines cross, it usually signifies an approaching change in the trend. When the indicator crosses down through the %D, it indicates the proximity of the closing price to the lowest low as compared to the last three sessions. We call this a bearish signal. The vice versa is a bullish signal.

The formula for calculating the stochastic indicator is;

$$\%K = \frac{recent\ closing\ price\ -\ lowest\ low}{highest\ high\ -\ lowest\ low} \times 100$$

The lowest low and highest high are of a certain period.

Typically, the indicator has fourteen periods, regardless of the timeframe. The fourteen-period setting implies the indicator line uses these three factors: the most recent closing price; the highest high over that period; and the lowest low over that period.

We mentioned that the stochastic indicator popularly trades bullish divergence, oversold conditions, bearish divergence, and overbought conditions.

The indicator can range from zero to a hundred, no matter how fast the price changes. A reading that is over 80 is a sign of an overbought condition, while under 20 is a sign of an oversold condition. Note, an oversold reading does not always have to be bullish, nor bearish for an overbought reading. The indicator can stay in the overbought or oversold area during an uptrend or downtrend, for a long period.

Divergences determine the tops and bottoms of trends. They also decide when it is appropriate to enter and exit a position. A divergence happens when the indicator and the price do not make lower lows or higher highs simultaneously. They diverge from each other. A bullish divergence occurs when the indicator forms a higher high while the price records a lower low. It may foreshadow a bullish reversal because it shows less downside momentum. A bearish divergence occurs when the indicator forms a lower high while the price records a higher high. It foreshadows a bearish reversal since there is less upside momentum.

The primary limitation of the indicator is producing false signals. This is when the indicator generates a trade signal, but the price does not follow through. It can lead to losing a trade.

### MACD: Moving Average Convergence and Divergence

MACD is a trend-following and trend-capturing indicator. It is an indication of the relationship which exists between two MAs belonging to the price of a security. Its calculation is the subtraction of the 26-period EMA from the 12-period EMA.

The MACD line is the result of the subtraction. A "signal line" is a nine-day EMA of the MACD. The signal line functions as a trigger for buying and selling signals when it is on top of the MACD line. Traders may buy or sell when the MACD crosses over the signal line or when it crosses under the line.

An EMA is a type of moving average that emphasizes recent data points. It is sometimes also known as Exponentially Weighted Moving Average. It has a higher reaction to price changes as compared to SMA. SMA gives equal significance to all changes in the period.

Whenever the 12-period EMA is above the 24-period, the MACD is positive. The MACD is negative whenever the 12-period is beneath the 24-period. The distance between the two EMAs grows, shown by how distant the MACD will be to the baseline, whether above or below.

The MACD is usually displayed with a histogram that graphs the distance between the MACD and the signal line. When the MACD line is over the signal line, the histogram is seen to be above the baseline. When MACD is beneath the signal line, the histogram is below the baseline. Traders use this histogram to know when the bearish or bullish momentum is high.

From the MACD histogram, two important terms emerge.

- **Convergence.** The histogram shrinks in size. It happens because there is a change in direction or the trend slows down. The MACD gets closer to the signal sign.

- **Divergence.** The histogram positively or negatively increases in height because the MACD accelerates faster in the current trend's direction.

The potential buy signal for the MACD histogram is when the histogram begins to converge to the zero line when it is below it. The potential sell signal is when the histogram converges to the line when it is above it.

MACD divergence is another way to interpret the MACD indicator. It has two forms. The first is a bearish divergence which occurs when the indicator suggests that a price should go down, but it instead continues its upward trend. The second is bullish divergence, which happens when the indicators suggest the price should head higher, but it continues its downward trend. The divergences can signal the trader to exit a position before the profits are lost.

Two of the limitations of MACD divergence is that it can sometimes create a false positive, and it does not forecast all reversals; that is, it does not predict a lot of real-life reversals. A false positive divergence happens when the price goes sideways following a trend. A sideways movement or slowdown in the momentum of the price may cause the MACD to move from the initial extremes, towards the zero lines, even without a true reversal.

### Average True Range

The average true range is an indicator used in trade analysis. It measures the volatility of the market. It does this through the decomposition of the range of a price during that given time. J. Welles Wilder Jr. introduced the indicator in his book "New Concepts in Technical Training."

The indicator is the greatest of:

- The current high is less than the current low
- The absolute value of the current high is less than the previous close
- The absolute value of the current low is less than the previous close

Generally using fourteen days, the ATR is said to be an MA of the true ranges.

To calculate the ATR, you find the true range value series for the security. The price range for the day is its low subtracted from its high. The true range is defined as:

$$TR = max[(high - low), abs(high - Cp), abs(low - Cp)]$$

$$ATR = \frac{1}{n}\left(\sum_{i=1}^{n} TR_i\right)$$

Where Tri is a true range and n is the period employed.

Originally, Wilde intended for the average true range to be used with commodities. However, the indicator also works well with stocks and indices. A stock, which experiences high volatility, has a relatively high ATR, while that with lower volatility will have a low ATR. Market technicians use the ATR to enter and exit trades. It allows traders to measure the volatility of assets accurately through simple calculations. The indicator, however, does not show the price direction. It mainly measures volatility generated by gaps and limits movement.

A common technique is the Chandelier Exit, which was brought about by Chuck LeBeau. A trailing stop is placed by the exit under the highest stock, where the distance between the stop and stock is at times an ATR multiple.

The ATR also gives traders indications of the size of trades to place on in markets. To position the sizing of a trade, traders can use the ATR. It takes into account a trader's inclination to accept the risk and volatility of the market.

The ATR has two main limitations. The first one is the subjective nature of the ATR, meaning it is can be interpreted differently by each trader. No ATR value assures a trader of a trend reversal or no reversal at all. Its readings have to be compared to previous ones to know if the trend is strong or weak.

The second limitation is that the ATR does not indicate the direction of the price. This may cause mixed signals, especially when the market experiences reversals or when trends are about to turn.

# CHAPTER 7
## PATTERNS

## DOUBLE BOTTOMS AND DOUBLE TOPS

### Double Bottoms

Double bottom patterns are technical analysis charting patterns that describe a change in trend and momentum reversal from the ongoing leading price action. The pattern describes a drop in the stock, a rebound, another drop to a similar level as the first drop, and another rebound. It resembles the letter "W."

Technical analysts believe that the first bottom should be a drop of about 10% to 20%. The second drop should be within 3 to 4% points of the prior low, increasing the volume of the coming advance.

This pattern is suited for the analysis of an intermediate-to-longer view of the market. The longer the duration between the lows, the greater the possibility that the pattern will be successful. Therefore, it is advisable to use daily or weekly price charts when analyzing the market for this pattern.

The pattern will always follow any downward trend, whether it is major or minor. It signals the reversal of the trend and the start of a potential uptrend. Consequently, the pattern must be validated, for the security itself by market fundamentals and the sector the security belongs to as well as the market itself. The fundamentals have to reflect the characteristics of the coming reversal in market conditions. The volume should also be closely monitored as the pattern forms. A spike in volume happens during the two upward prices. The spikes strongly indicate upward price pressure and serve as additional confirmation of a successful pattern.

Once the closing price is at the second rebound, approaching the first rebound's high, a long position can be taken at the price level of the first rebound's high, with a stop loss on the second loss. There should be a noticeable expansion in volume coupled with the fundamentals to indicate conducive market conditions for a reversal. Take a profit target above the entry price at two times the stop loss amount.

The main limitation when it comes to the double bottoms is that it is highly detrimental when interpreted incorrectly. One has to be patient and careful before jumping to any conclusions.

### Double Tops

Double tops are bearish technical reversal patterns. They form after an asset consecutively reaches a high price twice with some moderate decline in between the highs. The pattern completes once the price of the asset falls below the low between the two highs. A double top usually signifies a medium or long-term change in trend in an asset class.

There is a difference between a double top and a failed double top. A real double top is extremely bearish, which may lead to an extremely sharp decline in a trend. It is, however, important to have patience and identify the critical support level that confirms the identity of a double top. Basing the presence of a double top only on the formation of two consecutive peaks might lead to false reading and an early exit from the position.

Similar to double bottoms, the main limitation of double tops occurs when the pattern becomes misinterpreted.

### *Trading double tops and bottoms*

- **Trend identification.** To identify a double top pattern, observe a bullish trend. For a double bottom, identify a bearish trend. A pattern is unidentifiable in the absence of a trend. Though they can occur without trends, valid patterns exist within trends.

- **Creation of a top or low.** Each low within a bearish trend may be the beginning of a double bottom. Similarly, a top within a bullish trend may be the start of a double top. Carefully observe the price action at swings on a chart.

- **Trend interruption.** Observe if the price action interrupts the current trend. Normally, this will be in the form of the price action breaking the trend line.

- **Creation of a bottom or high.** For a double top, the creation of a bottom is necessary after the top. The bottom is on the bullish trend line, though this is not a necessity. For a double bottom, a high forms after the low.

- **Creation of the second top or low.** This is the re-test. The perfect double top will have its second top slightly lower than the first one, while the double bottom will have its low slightly higher than the first low. It shows that the trend is slowing down or is exhausted.

- **Drawing the neckline.** You draw the neckline by referencing the swing bottoms/highs, located between the two tops/lows. Then draw a horizontal line at that level.

- **Neckline breakout.** Confirm the validity of the pattern. The validity is confirmed if the price action closes a candle above the neckline or below it for a double bottom or double top respectively.

- **Trade entry**. After confirming the pattern, you have the go-ahead to enter the trade. For the double top, you open a small bearish trade, while for the double bottom a short bullish trade.

- **Stop loss.** Always secure your trade with a stop-loss order because there is no guarantee that the trade will always work in your favor. For the double top pattern, the optimal place to put your stop-loss is above the second top. For the double bottom, it's below the second low.

- **Size of the pattern.** Once you are short based on the pattern, you should project a possible target. You measure the size of the pattern and apply it starting from the neckline. This will be your minimum target. To measure the size of your pattern, connect the tops/bottoms in a single line. Add a perpendicular line, starting from the neckline to the line between the tops/bottoms. This distance is the size of your pattern.

- **Exit the trade.** It is advisable to exit the trade when the price action gets to the minimum target of the pattern.

## BEAR AND BULL FLAGS: HOW TO TRADE FLAG PATTERNS

The Flag pattern is a common and well-known continuation formation in trading. It is an on-chart figure and appears between impulsive legs of a trend as a minor consolidation. The presence of this pattern in a chart implies a high likelihood that the price action will break out in the prevailing trend's direction.

The flag pattern has two parts:

- **A flag pole.** It represents the trend impulse of the chart. Every trend impulse could appear in the form of a flag pole which brings the statement every trending move could transition into a flag.

- **A flag.** After the creation of the flag, a flag pattern will begin to trade within a tight range which takes the shape of the flag. The flag has price action with evenly distributed bottoms and tops. The price action is angled contrary to the trend impulse that creates the pole.

When you spot a flag pattern on the price chart, you will be equipped in measuring the approximate price target of the pattern. There are two targets that are related to the flag pattern:

- **Size of the flag.** The first target is from using the measured move technique. The measured move target is the distance equivalent to the size of the flag. To measure the flag size, you take the vertical distance between the upper channels and lower within the flag. You then apply this distance beginning from the breakout point. The first target is at the end of this distance.

- **Size of the flag pole.** To get the size of the pole, take the measurements of the vertical distance between the low and high of the pole. Apply the distance to the pattern starting from the breakout point.

For most traders, after the flag completes its targets, they opt to close out the position and bank their profits. Though for some instances, some may want to keep a small position open and ride out the larger trend move. Keeping a small position open is encouraged when there are signs of a strong trend even after the second target reaches. Ensure you manage the trade to determine a final exit point using price action-based clues.

A trend line indicator, for example, is useful in managing a possible runner. As long as the trend line is intact, you may decide to stay with the trade. Support and resistance rules are also important. When a price hits a level then bounces contrary to the trend, then the trend is getting exhausted. Otherwise, if the price breaks the level with increasing momentum, then it means the trend is getting stronger. Candlestick signals and chart patterns are other considerations. A reversal pattern is enough reason to close the trade and book your profits.

### Bear Flag Pattern

The pattern forms during bear trends. It begins with a bearish trend impulse, turning into a correction that directs upwards. During the correction phase, the bottoms and tops have an even distribution, and this creates a parallel channel.

The pattern completes when the price action breaks the flag boundary downwards. When this breakout happens, we have the chance to short the currency pair.

This pattern highlights a trading environment in which the supply and demand balance shifts in one direction of the market; that is, the supply is greater than the demand. This results in very little upward retracement allowing the flag pattern to take shape.

After the initial selloff, those who missed it will panic and start selling. More people begin selling during the flagpole stage. During the correction phase, they wait to get a higher price for them to sell. This, however, will not happen because the supply and demand equation is not balanced. We have another smash that makes people chase the move once more to the downside.

### Bull Flag Pattern

It is the opposite of the bear flag in terms of appearance. It forms during bull trends. It begins with a bullish trend move and turns into a small bearish correction whose top and bottom are parallel. The pattern completes with an upward breakout, and we prepare for a long position.

There are a few key things to note:

- The bull flag is most significant when appearing after a sharp advance in price.

- The flag can form over one or more weeks. The reliable ones take one to four weeks to form.

- Ideally, the lowest price point does not drop past the breakout point. If the price drops and continues past the breakout point, it can signal a change in the trend.

- Traders prefer waiting for the breakout to confirm that the trend is still in play. It is advisable not to anticipate a breakout. Consider the flag area as a "no trade zone."

### Trading the Flag Pattern

There are some rules and guidelines for effective trading with this pattern:

- **Flag Pattern trade entry.** Before entering a flag pattern trade, ensure you see the confirmation sign. The confirmation comes with the breakout. If you have a bull flag pattern, you buy when the price action closes the candle at the upper side. If you have a bear flag pattern, you sell when a candle closes below the lower level.

- **Flag pattern Stop loss.** Once you open your trade, you should position a stop-loss order. The order protects your trade from any unexpected price moves. If the price moves the opposite side of the breakout, then you should exit the trade since it means that the pattern is likely false. The logical position for the stop loss is beyond the most extreme swing that is within the flag pattern. If you have a bullish flag pattern, place the stop loss below the lowest bottom of the flag. If the pattern is a bear flag, place it above the highest top in the flag.

- **Flag Pattern Take profit.** The take profit for this pattern is addressed using the targets discussed above. It is upon you to decide which target to pursue. Experienced traders often suggest taking profits at both targets to reduce the risks and book profits.

## BEAR AND BULL PENNANTS

A pennant is an entry pattern for the continuation of a trend that is already established. The formation happens after a sharp price movement that contains gaps, also known as the mast or pole, where the pennant represents a period of uncertainty and indecision at the middle point of the full move, consolidating the previous leg. A small symmetric triangle contains the price. The triangle begins wide and converges to a point as the pattern progresses.

The pattern is complete when the price breaks away from the triangle along the direction of the preceding trend. At this point, the price is likely to continue in that direction. Conservative traders will look for more confirmation that the trend will continue. A common stop level is on the opposite side of the breakout just outside the pennant. Pennants and triangles should not be mistaken to be the same as they are distinct price patterns.

### Bull Pennants

Bull pennants are one of the most popular patterns, especially among long bias traders. During consolidation, the trading has converging trend lines. Some traders say that the consolidation period is the optimum time to enter a trade.

In this pattern, the pennant part is more of a wedge part on top of the flagpole. After the flagpole forms, the wedge moves to form the pennant look. The flagpole is normally bullish candlesticks, either made of a big one or several together. This formation occurs because the flagpole shows a large volume coming in, while the pennant has a low or weakening volume.

Bull pennant patterns occur when the stock breaks resistance. Candlesticks and moving averages are important in these cases as they form the key levels and become important signals for buying and selling. Drawing correct trend lines is also important when it comes to trading, not just with the bullish pennant pattern. Incorrectly drawn trend lines could mess up your entry points and reduce your chances of a successful trade.

To trade the bull pennants, you need to observe the patterns together with the candlestick. You also need confirmation of the continuation of the pattern, as well as the volume coming in. the bodies and wicks of the candlesticks together with trend lines, form the resistance. If the pattern breaks down shortly after breaking the resistance, you may want to go short or take your profit depending on your point of entry. Do not, however, think that every pattern will behave the same every time. Each point in the market is unique.

### Bear Pennants

Bear pennant is a price action pattern that follows a spontaneous move in the market. It is a representation of short consolidation proceeded by the continuing of the prior bearish trend. Visually, a bear pennant has two parts: a pole that has a base and tip, and a pennant similar to a small symmetric triangle facing right, attached to the pole. The pole looks like it is upside down and has its tip at the bottom.

They are characterized by lower lows and higher lows series and have trend lines representing the support and resistance. The shape is usually changing by the slopes of the downward resistance line and the upward support line which converge towards each other.

The bear pennant pattern has three phases:

- Background. This is a strong thrusting action, that has an increase in volume and price, which forms a distinct view of the direction of a bearish trend. Its representation is a downward pointing tip. The pole is important in recognizing the possible continuation of the pattern. It is also a representation of the direction of the trend and the strength of the trend.

- The second phase is for the action consolidation in terms of volume and also price. Its representation is the Pennant. Traders prefer seeing this second phase short with about two or three swings as the price action remains within the range and has the lower highs and higher lows shape, with constant volume.

- The pattern is confirmed if the action forms another bearish trend which has a surge in price and volume. The lower support shown by Pennant is where traders observe and confirm the trend. The action normally mimics the volatility and energy that comes with the Pole creation.

## DIFFERENCES BETWEEN FLAG AND PENNANT

The main difference between the Flag and Pennant is the shape of the correction that comes after the Pole.

The Flag pattern forms a channel correction, while the Pennant forms a triangle correction. Otherwise, the two patterns are similar, with the same rules for trading applying to both.

## ABCD PATTERNS

ABCD pattern is a harmonic pattern from which every other pattern derives. The pattern has three price swings. The AB and CD lines are the "legs." The BC line is a correlation or retracement. The lines AB and CD have the same size.

A bullish ABCD pattern is one that follows a downward trend and is likely to have a reversal to the upside. A bearish ABCD pattern forms after an upward trend and is a sign of a potential bearish reversal at some level. You need to take into account the pattern's direction and the movement of the market it will predict.

There are three types of ABCD patterns:

- **Classic ABCD pattern.** Using the Fibonacci retracement tool on AB, point C should be between 61.8% and 78.6% of AB. The point D should be between 127.2% and 161.8% of BC. Note that the 61.8% retracement at C will result in the 161.8% projection of BC, while the 78.6% will result in a 127% projection.

- **AB=CD pattern.** AB and CD have the same length. The market takes equal time to travel from A to B and C to D, resulting in AB and CD having the same angle. This pattern type is popular among traders.

- **ABCD extension.** The line CD, in this case, is the 127.2% to 161.8% extension of line AB. CD can be two or more times larger than AB. A gap after point C or the presence of big candlesticks near C are some of the hints that CD will be longer than AB.

### How to trade ABCD pattern

It is important to remember that you can only enter the trade after the price has arrived at point D. study the chart and look for the highs and lows of the price. Using the Zigzag indicator might help mark the chart's swings.

Watch the price while it forms AB and BC. If the pattern is bullish, point C must be lower than point A and be the intermediate-high after point B. Point D will be a new low below point B. When the market arrives at D, use some trading techniques to ensure that the price is reversed up, or down if the pattern is bearish. The best scenario for this is a reversed candlestick pattern. A buy order will probably be set at point D, at or above the candle's high.

### Importance of the ABCD Pattern

- It assists in identifying opportunities in markets, in any condition and timeframe.

- It is the basis of all other patterns.

- At the completion of the pattern is the highest probability of trade entry.

- It helps in determining the risk vs the reward before placing a trade.

- Several patterns converge to form a strong trade signal.

## HEAD AND SHOULDERS PATTERNS

It is a formation in the chart, which is similar to a baseline with three peaks. The two peaks outside are close in terms of height while the middle peak is the highest. Trade experts believe that this particular pattern is one of the dependable trend reversal patterns.

The pattern forms when the price of a stock rises to a peak and declines to the base before the up-move. The price then rises above the former peak and once again declines to the original base. Finally, the price rises again to the level of the initial peak before declining to the base of the pattern one more time. The first and last peaks are the shoulders. The second peak is the head. The neckline is the line that connects the first and last troughs.

Whether the price of a stock increases or decreases is the result of how many people are on which team. Bulls are people who believe that the price will go up, while bears are those who believe that it will go down. If the majority of the stakeholders are bulls, the price will go up since new investors will buy in to take advantage of the opportunity. If more stakeholders are bears, then the price will go down because they will sell the shares to avoid losing their money.

### Inverse Head and Shoulders

It is the opposite of the head and shoulder and is also known as the head and shoulders bottom. It predicts reversals in downward trends.

It happens when the stock's price falls to a trough then rises. The price then falls below the initial trough and rises again. Finally, the price once again falls to the level of the initial fall. After the final trough, the price moves upward towards the top of the prior troughs.

The inverse pattern mirrors the head and shoulder pattern. It has a bullish outlook as opposed to the bearish outlook of the head and shoulder pattern.

### Head and Shoulders Pattern Rules

- **Draw the pattern.** The bottom created after the head forms is the first sign of the pattern. The bottom will likely slow down the trend's intensity. The two tops increase and correspond to the bullish trend. The bottom, however, is created after the head breaks the trend line and ends somewhere close to the previous bottom. This shows that the bullish momentum is slowing down. We then anticipate the third top, which is at par with the first one.

- **Neckline.** The head and shoulders neckline is said to be the most important aspect. The neckline is manually drawn by locating the two bottoms and joining them with a line. The line could be horizontal or declined, depending on the chart pattern. On rare occasions, it can also be declined.

- **Breakout.** A breakout is a sign we need to open a short trade. A valid breakout is when the price breaks through the neckline of the pattern. When a candle closes just below the neckline, it triggers a short signal for the pattern's setup.

- **Stop loss.** The head and shoulders trade goes hand in hand with a stop-loss order. Since it is not 100% successful, there is a need to protect trading accounts. For optimal results, the order is put on the second shoulder.

### Advantages of the Head and Shoulders Pattern

- It is easily identifiable for more experienced traders.

- It defines the risks and takes the profit levels.

- It has the potential to exploit big market movements.

- It is useful in every market.

### Limitations of Head and shoulders Pattern

- Novice traders find it difficult to identify the pattern.

- The price sometimes can pull back and retest the neckline which confuses beginner traders.

- The risk-reward rations may not always be favorable.

# CHAPTER 8

## SWING TRADING GUIDING PRINCIPLES

### THE ROUTINE OF A SWING TRADER

For a trader to be successful in their trade swinging, they need to spend a good amount of time on the markets analyzing and finding the loopholes. The first thing they need to do is begin their day slightly earlier than the opening time of the markets, that is before the opening bell, which is rung at 6 am EST. This will help them get a general overview of what is expected and the things that should go into their watch list of the day, the potential trades they can cash in, and the existing positions of the different trading instruments.

### Market Overview

The second step is to look at the latest news across the world, that is both economically and politically to see what role these fundamental factors are likely to play during the day's trading time. This is because according to the fundamental analysts, if there is a negative change in the political or economic structure of a certain nation or region, the odds of the currency of the affected areas going low are very high and the traders would like to have a step ahead in this so they can sell off and cut down on their losses. The trader can catch up on this news using either reliable websites such as Market watch or watching television cable networks such as CNBC. While doing this, the trader should pay attention to three things; in particular, they include:

1. **The market sentiment**—this is the general feel of the market pattern that could either be bearish or bullish, it also involves looking out for the inflation fluctuations in the national currency and reading the economic reports that may have been released.

2. **Sector sentiment**—this is the general feel of the different economic sectors that make up an economy, such as the manufacturing sector, the agricultural sector etcetera. The general sectoral composition of an economy will tell the trader what the best move to make on a currency is. For instance, if the manufacturing sector of an economy is growing, the likelihood of the currency being strong is greater than the economy which is majorly focused on the agricultural sector

3. **Current portfolio contents**—the trading instruments in the current portfolio of a market are vital to any swing trader since they get to know what is hot on the market and vice versa. The news that is put forth on either futures or options, earnings, and regulations will come in handy when the trader has to make a decision.

### Potential Trades

After a swing trader has conducted their market overview research and is armed with the findings from this analysis, they are now set to scan for the potential trades they can engage in during the day. Normally, a swing trader will use the fundamental analysis to scan for the right entry positions before they apply their own technical analysis to get the perfect exit points. The three main methods swing traders utilize in getting the right fundamental catalysts for their entry points to include:

## SPECIAL OPPORTUNITIES

These are moments such as initial public offerings, mergers, acquisitions, and suspensions, takeovers and buyouts, bankruptcy announcements, insider buying, and restructuring, among other things. In such moments the swing trader will most likely do the opposite of what the trend is, they will buy when the trend is selling and sell when the trend is buying.

## SECTOR PLAYS

This is similar to what the trade did in the market overview; they pay attention to certain sectors and hop on to the train as it embarks on its journey. Whenever a sign of a retracement appears the swing traders will alight the train since all they needed to do was ride the trend when it was perfect for them.

## CHART BREAKS

By analyzing the charts, swing traders will always note the different trading instruments that will be close to a resistance or support level. They will utilize patterns such as;

### Symmetrical Triangle patterns

This is a continuation pattern that has at least two higher highs and lows and two lower lows.

#### THE LOGIC BEHIND THE SYMMETRICAL TRIANGLE PATTERN

Buyers will push the price in different directions as the sellers. The buyers will keep pushing the price up, making it higher, and the sellers will equally push the price low making lower highs. This kind of narrowing of the trading range usually means that the buyers and sellers are both losing interest in that price level, and they may feel as though the security or pair is overrated. This explains why the pattern starts wide and begins to narrow towards the end of the pattern. When the trading range begins to narrow when either the buyers or sellers were having a kind of war, it signals the possibility of a big sharp move in either direction depending on who caves first among the buyers and sellers breaking the pattern. The narrowing also means there are low volumes of orders in the market at that specific level, since, the buyer considers the price level unattractive for them to purchase and the seller feels the price is not that attractive for him to sell either. However, when the price breaks out of this small range, it will move fast in one direction, all we can do as traders is wait prepared for the pattern to break in our predetermined direction of trade and with a stop order in the other direction because we must prepare for the worst even as we hope for the best.

## Ascending Triangle Pattern

This is a bullish continuation pattern that must have at least two highs and two lows that can be connected with more than one trend line. The top most trend line will have to be horizontal while the lower trend line has to be diagonal.

### THE LOGIC BEHIND ASCENDING TRIANGLE PATTERNS

The logic behind this continuation pattern is pretty obvious, and I am sure you can already tell what it is. If you thought that the sellers are not going down without a fight and the buyers are still breathing down their necks persistently, then you are right. The buyers will push the price higher making higher lows while the sellers insist on keeping the prices low at the level where the horizontal trend line is. Unfortunately, or fortunately, depending on what your predetermined direction is, the sellers will cave in and admit defeat and stop entering sell orders at the horizontal line since the buyers will counteract that move and push the price back up to the levels where they sold and triggered their stop losses. With this outnumbering of the sellers, the buyers will be in control of the market. After this spiff, the pattern will break, and the trend will resume the trend that had been established by the previous impulsive move.

### Descending triangle pattern

This is a continuation pattern that is literally the opposite of the ascending triangle pattern. It is a bearish continuation pattern which means that the trend is down and the price will have to stop for a short period of time in order to consolidate, and this type of move forms a descending triangle pattern before the trend resumes going further down.

### THE LOGIC BEHIND DESCENDING TRIANGLE PATTERNS

This logic behind this particular pattern mirrors the one that is behind ascending triangle patterns. In this case, though the sellers are in large numbers and the trend is moving down. The buyers will hold their forte and keep it down at the horizontal trend line. Although this will only last a short period of time before the sellers, who are in the majority, win and break the pattern leading to a resumption of the trend downwards.

### Price Channel

This is a continuation pattern that is made up of two parallel trend lines, that is one above and the other below the price that takes the shape of a channel. This is a continuation pattern that is applicable in both the bullish and bearish markets. The distinction between these two markets is the direction in which the sloping will occur. If the channel slopes upwards, then this is considered a bullish continuation pattern and vice versa if the channel is sloping downward then we can consider this the bearish continuation pattern. Like the rest of the patterns, the trend lines have to be drawn while connecting at least two highs and two lows.

### THE LOGIC BEHIND THE PRICE CHANNEL CONTINUATION PATTERN

- When the trend is up:

This means the buyers are in control in this case and the price will stop in order for it to consolidate when they eventually decide to take some of the profits out of the market, but in that specific moment, the sellers will be out of sight. The sellers are weak in this case and lack the strength to correct the trend or even make a minute move against the trend direction. Therefore, the price will just trickle on upwards, slowly forming a channel before the buyers eventually resume the strong trend by breaking the already slow-moving pattern and taking the movement further higher. This is the bullish price channel continuation pattern.

- When the trend is down:

The vice versa of what happens in the bullish price channel continuation pattern will occur here since it is a bearish type of continuation pattern when the trend is moving down. In this case, it means the sellers are in control and the price will stop in order for it to consolidate when they eventually decide to take some of the profits out of the market but in that specific moment, the buyers will be out of sight. The buyers who are weak in this case will equally lack the strength to correct the trend or even make a minute move against the trend direction, therefore, the price will just trickle on downwards slowly forming a channel before the sellers eventually resume the strong trend by breaking the already slow-moving pattern and taking the movement further lower.

## CREATING A WATCH LIST

Swing traders should now create a watch list after the analysis of the different currencies they would like to keep an eye on. It is advisable for the list to have columns that show the target prices, the entry prices, and the stop-loss prices of each trading instrument.

## LOOK AT THE EXISTING POSITIONS

The traders must look at the positions that they are in at this pre-market hour before the opening bell sounds. With the fundamental analysis report at the back of their minds, they need to pay attention to the changes that are likely to be influenced, and if they stand to gain or lose their current positions. This is important because it always guides the trader on whether they should adjust either their stop-loss signals or their take-profit positions in order to adjust to the recent changes.

### Market Hours

Once the opening bell sounds, the swing traders will look at who is buying and who is selling. They focus on the trend and plan their entry and exit using different analyses as discussed below.

### Flag pattern trade example

Let us assume the last impulsive move on the four-hour chart was down, when we check the thirty-minute chart we will have to wait for a continuation pattern to form. After it forms, we will wait for the price to break in the direction of the impulsive move on the four-hour chart. In this case, when the move was down, we are going to be seeking to sell, so we need the flag to break on the downside. Break-in this case means zooming out of the 30-minute chart and waiting for a thirty-minute candle to form and close outside below the flag pattern after this candle has closed out, zooming out of the thirty minutes chart, and waiting for the price to go back up to the red lower trend line and retest it (get close to it.) this will now be a Resistance line. When a pattern breaks and the price comes back shortly to retest the line, this is what forms a resistance line. We should enter the sell stop order at the level where the price started to rise back up and retest the lower trend line of the flag. The Stop loss is placed where the retest of the trend line took place.

## How to Manage the Stop Loss level

In the example above, when the price begins to move away from the flag pattern, it will form small lower highs! We should trail our stop loss levels manually to just above these lower highs.

There are two ways to enter the trade; the first one is the method discussed above where we wait for the re-test of the pattern and the second one is to enter when a thirty-minute candle body is completely outside the pattern if the retest did not happen right after the first candle that closed outside it. The reason is that at times the trend will be too strong and the retest may never happen as speculated before.

### *Descending triangle trade example*

Let us assume there is a clear downtrend with the most recent impulsive move on the four-hour chart moving down. The pattern then breaks to the downside as we would like it to break but after the first thirty minutes the candle closes tight outside our pattern and there is no retest on the lower trend line. If there is no retest after the first candle that breaks the pattern, then we should enter at the close of the second candle that is considerably outside the pattern. We should not wait for the retest as it did not happen after the first candle chances are it will not happen now either, we should place the stop loss above the last minor lower high that is inside the pattern. After that, we shall manually trail the stop-loss order as we did in the previous example where we entered the order after the patterns reset

### Ascending triangle trade example

Let us assume there is a clear uptrend with the most recent impulsive move on the four-hour chart moving up, but there is no retest after the first candle that closes above the pattern. We will have to enter the trade at the close of the second candle, which should be completely out of the pattern. It is imperative to do this and make some pips instead of sitting around waiting on a retest that may very much not appear.

### Rectangle pattern trade example

After the broken candle closes outside the pattern, the retest of the resistance lines is put into play. We should enter the market when the price comes back down at the close of the breakout candle and set the stop loss in the places where the retest finished, and the prices started going down and away from the pattern and trend.

## EXITS

One of the exit strategies we have touched on is the stop-loss method where you can trail it manually to points just above the lower highs on the thirty-minute chart when selling or just below the higher knows if you are the buyer. These are considered the logical turning points in the market. They are the least likely levels that the price will touch whenever there is a strong direction, and this makes them a perfect spot to hang the stop loss.

The second way to exit the trade earlier than this moment involves the wedge continuation pattern. We agreed that the wedge pattern could be either a continuation or a reversal pattern, and this depends on the location that the wedge is in. Just a reminder, if the wedge pattern forms at the correction phase of a huge trend on the four-hour chart and it slopes against the trend, then this is a continuation pattern, and we can use it to enter trades. The wedge pattern can also emerge in the impulsive moves of the trend, indicating that the trend is about to come to a stop. The slope of the pattern, in this case, should be in line with the trend. The moment you spot this pattern emerging, you should keep an eye out for the breaking of the trend, which is the confirmation of the end of the said trend.

The main approach for trade exists still remains the manual trailing of stop-loss either below or above the logical points. However, if you see a wedge that will break to the downside if the last impulsive move is an uptrend or breaks to the upside if the last impulsive move on the four-hour chart is a downside then you as the trader should exit when the pattern breaks and a 30-minute candle forms outside to signify the end of the trend. This is actually a better exit level since you do not need to wait for the price rise till it gets to the last high or go down to the last low so that your stop loss level is hit and the order materializes eating away at a small part of your profits.

### Head and Shoulders pattern

This is a trend formation that shows a reversal and is formed by a certain peak which is considered a shoulder and then followed by a taller peak which is ahead, and a shorter peak (shoulder) follows suit, and so on so forth. When the lowest points of two troughs are connected by a line, this line is called the neckline. The neckline can either slope down or upwards. When the line slopes down, it indicates a more reliable signal. A target can be calculated by measuring the distance from the neckline to the topmost point of the head in the chart. This difference is a representation of how far the price will move up after it goes past the neckline. It is also the same distance that the price will make once it falls below the neckline.

At the end of the day, traders should always remember that they should not adjust their positions to take on more risk. They should instead make adjustments to either lock in profits or to take in more profit-taking levels.

### After Hours Market

After trading doing the day, traders are required to do a performance evaluation after the closing time of the markets. The report should have a good and clear recording of the trades that have either won or lost during the day. These reports will be used for both monitoring the performance and evaluating it as well as in the case of tax compliance. After the evaluations, traders are required to record their closing positions of all the open trades while paying close attention to the announcements that have been made after hours in order to help them in their pre-market analysis the following day.

The routine of a swing trader shows that one needs to plan diligently and prepare properly since the pre-market hours help them identify the potential trades and market opportunities of the day, the market hours are then spent enacting the conclusions that were drawn in the morning on the different positions and the after-hours are for evaluating the day's work and ensuring that the same thing that was written down in theory still happened practically.

## HOW TO SCAN FOR SWINGING TRADE

This involves the use of a market radar which literally shows the trader where their counterparts are and what their moves are. The market radars can be easily incorporated into the different market scanners that are available all over the internet. We will discuss five different market radars that the trader can incorporate into their market scanners so that they do not miss out on any trading opportunity.

### ADX Trend Scan

This is a swinging trading strategy that is also known as finding the Holy Grail. It involves looking for retracements within any trend that is considered perfect and healthy. For the long traders, they are required to use a 30-period ADX which should be indicating that it is above 30 and still going higher, their retracement levels should be a 20 simple moving average that the price should hit, once the price hits here, the traders should now order at the topmost point of the bar that is in contact with the 20 periods simple moving average. The short-term traders should use a 14-period ADX that is also above thirty and keeps on climbing higher; their retracement level should also be at the 20-period simple moving average, however, when the bar touches the simple moving average, the trader should sell at the lowest point that is in contact.

### ADX Range Trades Galore

This is the indicator that looks around at the sideways moving markets for different trade setups such as the Gimmee Bar which is a market entry trading strategy that has the trader looking for a reversal pattern that is moving from the highest point of a trading range or the vice versa. From the long trader's point of view, the Gimmee bar trading strategy has prices that are considered to be going down and losing in a trading range. These prices should further touch the lower Bollinger band and form another bar that will always end at a higher position than the initial start-up position. This bar is known as the Gimmee bar that the trader should then consider buying just slightly above. The short-term traders, on the other hand, will deal with prices that will be seen as rising and going up in a trading range and touching the higher Bollinger band. They should then form another bar that will always end at a point that is considerably lower than the position where it opened, this bar known as the Gimmee bar is the spot that indicates where traders should sell at. The spot should be just slightly below this bar. However, should this bar cross and overlap the Moving average, or record a much wider range than the other Bollinger bands and bars, or alternatively open and go further than the range of the bars, the trader is advised to let go and not trade with the Gimmee bars. Whenever the ADX increases, it shows that the trend is supposedly getting stronger while the slight motion of the ADX in a downward trend will indicate the trading ranges required for analysis.

### Hull Moving Average

While most of the traders are only aware of two moving averages, the Hull moving average is considered an exotic MA that helps the traders scan the waves in the markets and charts. Once the Hull Moving Average has been drawn on a chart, it is most likely to be way smoother than the actual market price while still flowing with the different ups and downs in the markets that form waves. The trader is advised to track down these turning points and use them to analyze the market waves and see the reversals and continuations likely to come up. If the slope of the Hull Moving Average is positive, then the trend that is being implied is the bull swing which is just stating and vice versa, if the slope is negative then the trend that has begun is known as the bear swing.

### Extreme Volume

If the volume is high, the odds of the trends ending or new trending breaking out are very high. Bollinger

bands that have been thoroughly explained in the previous chapter are some of the best indicators of finding
the excessive trade volumes in a market to enable the
swing traders to learn. Large trading volumes always
lead to the appearance of exhaustion gaps, which usually appear immediately after the trend has come to
a stop. It is caused by an increase of the last-minute
buyers who get into a bullish market at the end of the
trend right before the reversal commences. The gap
will always close after about five different bars. Therefore, this is the windfall that the swing traders should
look for if they want to make the move that they need
to cash in their profits.

### Impulse system scan

The first rule of trading usually does not trade against
the trend; the other rule of swing trading does not
trade against the impulse system momentum. That
is considered a suicidal move that will most likely land
you in a series of bad trades that will make you lose a
lot. The impulse system scan uses a combination of two
indicators that is the Moving Average Convergence Divergence and the Exponential Moving Average to scan
the market and figure out its momentum. According
to researchers, when these two indicators cross, that
is the implication of an impulsive move that is often
found in the trading psychology of human beings. The
higher the time frame that the trader employs in this
specific moment, the better and improve their trading
set up will be. A long-term trader who is using a 13 period should have the exponential moving average in a
rising pattern and the (12,26,9) Moving Average Convergence Divergence indicator forming a histogram that
seems to be going higher too. These positions should
encourage the trader should get into the market. The
short-term trader should use the same indicators as
well, but the difference is the indicators should show a
position that is going lower. This is a colored indicator

that has the blue color scheme code which indicates the disagreeing session of both indicators, the green color scheme should show a positive impulse which is ideal for long term traders and the red color scheme indicates the negative impulse systems which means the prices are falling which is perfect for short term traders.

## HOW TO BUY LOW AND SELL HIGH

When it comes to trading, you will realize that it does not just understand that basics like you would go to the market to get your apple. The first thing that you will need is a frame of reference. You should have a technique on a chart that helps you understand that this is relatively low priced hence the possible time to enter the trade. You will need two methods if you want to make it a trade entry.

You will need support and a resistant chart to help you know when it is time to enter the market. With this, you will look back historically to know where there is a low price. You, therefore, work on the probability of knowing where the resistance and supports are. You also need a confirmation of the market before you buy. You should not just buy because the prices are low. Look for a sign of strength where the candle has a bullish close. You will find that the buyers are stepping in here and there is a good chance that the market could hit higher.

When you want to sell, you should be looking for high prices; thus, you need to know the high price area from your chart. You also need to note the high cost that you are targeting. You will note that sometimes the swing pattern will get shorter and shorter. You will, therefore, use the pattern. You will ask yourself on what level of the chart is there an opposing pressure that is coming in and that will go against your trade. You know that sellers come in at swing highs, resistance, or at a previous support time resistance. If you want to make it, then you need to sell on a low swing level as you will be able to make more at that point.   It is a minor support period, and it may become resistant. That is the best place to exit the trade on one swing of the market. Pay attention to the first level that swings high and take your partial profits. Sellers may be looking for areas of reasonable prices since there is a good chance that the market could reverse from there.

# CONCLUSION

Swing Trading is a type of trading that is carried out in the Forex markets, especially by traders who have slightly busy schedules or prefer a short-term trading period. Contrary to popular belief, making money in the Forex market is not easy, losing money on the other hand is very easy. The right attitude to either a loss or a gain is the difference between successful traders and unsuccessful traders. If the trader follows their impulses and guts, the odds of ending up bankrupt are much higher than for the trader who does extensive analysis and uses the information to either get into the market or get off a certain trend.

The first part to remember is that you should be aware of the terminologies. You do not want to be on a different page when people are discussing something completely different. You should also ensure that you know what time it is and what is happening in the forex market at that particular time. For example, we know that the best time to trade is when there is an overlap in the London and New York time zones. Therefore, your daily alarms and reminders must coincide with this. You will do well to comply with these instructions to make the maximum profits. You could also trade within the other hours that are outside the advised and make a standard amount of return. It's all a game of wits. You will always do what is best for you.

It is also important to stress the fact that you need to keep up with world news. These are the decisions that decide whether a certain currency remains strong or sells at a loss. This, in turn, goes to inform your choices on whether to trade using a particular pair. It prepares you for what to expect when trading that day. This is similar to going outside and realizing that a particular road is closed due to certain reasons. This will inform you of what routes to use to arrive at your destination. The same thing happens with the knowledge that comes from world news. Governments are key players in controlling the direction the financial markets take. Pay close attention and get to save yourself the agony of losing hard-earned money. Going against the trend has proven to be detrimental to most trades. Thus the famous trading saying "The trend, is your friend".

Understanding the psychology of trading is your number one job before embarking on any trade. Sometimes you will lose, sometimes you will gain. Throughout these motions, you will require a lot of discipline. You need to understand that losing should not kick you out of the game. Making good profits does not also act as an invitation to place bigger lot sizes that could clean you out. Achieving balance and a clear head is a hard task but the best traders understand how vital it is. As a trader, it is your duty to sit back and analyze your actions after a trade and fish out the lessons learned. It is advisable to keep a trading journal. It will go a long way to keeping you accountable and on top of the game.

This is a business just like any other. Everyone in business needs a strategy that helps them maximize profits and avoid major losses. Without this, you are just gambling and stand a high chance of losing your money and falling into depression. Study this book over and over again, get to familiarize yourself with forex trading. Start trading on a dummy account where you can put everything to test and become good. After this, you can safely graduate into the actual market where you can trade real currencies in real-time. It is healthy to involve yourself with communities and societies that are into forex trading. Get to share your own experiences and learn from others. You can ask questions and get advice on how to become the best in your trading journey. There are many advantages of swing trading in forex as discussed in this book. Take advantage while you can. Gather as much information as you can and start practicing. Your output will always be directly proportional to your input.

**IF YOU LIKE THIS BOOK, HELP ME BY LEAVING A REVIEW ON AMAZON!**

Scan the QR code with your mobile phone and you can immediately leave a review,

Or

1. Go to **Amazon** and click on "**My orders**"
2. Search for **this book** and click to go into details
3. Scroll down and click on    Write a customer review

Share the pages you liked the most with and post them in the reviews.

Thanks a lot! See you soon.
**Mark Swing**

To make sure you **don't miss any new book**, **follow my Author page on Amazon**

https://www.amazon.com/Mark-Swing/e/B082M-MQ6SM/ref=dp_byline_cont_pop_book_1

Or scan this QR code with your mobile phone

Manufactured by Amazon.ca
Acheson, AB

10599910R00146